Halfway to Justice

One man's fight to bring his daughter's murderer to justice.

Ken Turner and Lesley Turner

NEW
HOLLAND

First published in Australia in 2005 by
New Holland Publishers (Australia) Pty Ltd
Sydney • Auckland • London • Cape Town

14 Aquatic Drive Frenchs Forest NSW 2086 Australia
218 Lake Road Northcote Auckland New Zealand
86 Edgware Road London W2 2EA United Kingdom
80 McKenzie Street Cape Town 8001 South Africa

10 9 8 7 6 5 4 3 2 1 / 2 4 6 8 10 9 7 5 3 1

National Library of Australia Cataloguing-in-Publication Data:

   Turner, Ken L.
   Halfway to justice.
   Bibliography.
   ISBN 1 74110 249 9.

   1. Fathers of murder victims - Australia - Biography. 2.
   Murder victims' families - Australia - Biography. 3.
   Victims of crimes - Australia. I. Turner, Lesley L. II.
   Title.
   362.88092

Managing Editor: Monica Berton
Editor: Jacqueline Blanchard
Designer: Jo Buckley
Production Assistant: Kellie Masterson
Printed in Australia by McPherson's Printing Group, Victoria

The authors and publishers have made every effort to ensure the information in this book
was correct at the time of going to press and accept no responsibility for any errors that may
have occurred. Every effort has been made to trace original source material in this book.
Where the attempt has been unsuccessful, the publishers would be pleased to hear from the
copyright holder to rectify any omission.

'You looked so beautiful when you came into this world
my one ray of sunshine, daddy's little girl,
your pretty smile and your eyes so blue,
kisses and cuddles are my memories of you.'

Ken Turner and Gary B

 **Preface**

This book questions how the criminal justice system can be said to deliver justice to victims given its failing and perceived inadequacies in the circumstances described in this book. Yet the answers and preferred options are not always self-evident. What we can find in this tale is something of the true human spirit, both in Shirree's will to live and her father's desire to seek true justice for his daughter. I admire his strength in the telling of his story.

Dr Rick Sarre
Legal commentator, University of South Australia

Contents

Acknowledgments 7

Chapter 1 **My Little Girl** 11

Chapter 2 **Tears of Distress** 17

Chapter 3 **A Public Goodbye** 33

Chapter 4 **A Kind Of Healing** 53

Chapter 5 **A Break in the Case** 65

Chapter 6 **The Committal Hearing** 73

Chapter 7 **Waiting** 87

Chapter 8 **The Crown vs Mercuri** 93

Chapter 9 **What's Wrong With the Truth?** 107

Chapter 10 **Unreliable Witnesses** 119

Chapter 11 **The Accused** 135

Chapter 12 **Innocent?** 147

Chapter 13 **The Verdict** 167

Chapter 14 **Pursuing Justice** 175

Chapter 15 **Media Attention** 187

Chapter 16 **Politics and the Law** 195

Chapter 17 **Halfway to Justice** 209

Epilogue **Not a Fairytale Ending** 227

A Word from the Author 235

Endnotes 239

Acknowledgments

There are many people whom I must thank. There were members of my family and friends who gave me so much support and encouragement through this whole ordeal and continue to do so. So, where do I begin? I don't think it is wise to name individuals because there will always be at least one who is missed and I don't want to leave anybody out. It will be sufficient to say that they know who they are and they know how grateful I am for all of their support.

I want to thank the State Government of South Australia, and the Attorney-General's Department for approving the reward of $100,000 for information leading to the conviction of Shirree's killer.

I acknowledge gratefully the kindness and consideration extended by Justice EP Mullighan and the Sheriff's Officers, Supreme Court, Magistrate's Court and District Court Staff of Adelaide.

I am very grateful for the courtesy extended to me from the media. I want to thank all involved both locally and nationally for the coverage that was given throughout the entire case. I was able to develop special friendships with some of the media representatives.

To my good friend Steve Condous who hates injustice as much as I do. Thank you so much for your encouragement and support.

To the Director of Public Prosecutions, Paul Rofe QC, whose task it was to prosecute the case in the criminal court. Paul, you did the best you could with what you had to work with under extremely frustrating circumstances. I will always be grateful to you for your patience with me when I pestered you with question after question that couldn't be answered easily.

I will be forever grateful to the police officers and detectives who worked tirelessly on the investigation through most difficult circumstances. Especially to Detective Senior Sergeant Michael Johnson, who had the full responsibility of conducting the investigation, I can never adequately thank you for your support and encouragement. When the investigation was leading nowhere you didn't give up, your dogged determination to find Shirree's killer was never in question. You always knew you would get your man in the end.

To the Victims of Crime support group who were there when I needed them—thank you. To Dr Ann Williams, who kept me from sinking further into the depths of depression—I will always appreciate how you gently showed me that what I was going through was a very normal reaction to an abnormal circumstance and I wasn't going insane.

To the staff at Tindall, Gask & Bentley I offer my undying gratitude for your patience, understanding, support and encouragement. I will never be able to thank Ron Bentley enough for taking on my case in the first place, even though a case of this type had never been attempted before in Australia. When I needed a pro-active firm of lawyers to embrace the pursuit of justice you were willing to take on this groundbreaking case without reservation.

To Andrew Martin QC, whom I did not know for long but who worked so hard to prepare the case for presentation in the Civil Court, I am very grateful for the work you did.

How can I possibly express adequately how I feel about Morry Bailes and Brendan Connell? I will never forget their tireless efforts to present the very best case possible, one which I know would have succeeded had we been given the right circumstances to see it all the way through to the end. I will be forever grateful for their total belief that justice must prevail in all circumstances. No words can adequately express my gratitude for their endless encouragement and support and the excellent work they did in the preparation of the civil action.

What do I say to you, Lesley? When the challenge was presented you grabbed it with both hands. I value so much your strong opinions and your willingness to do the hard yards. I saw the awesome amount of research you put into this project. I will always be grateful for your dedication.

Finally, to my son Bradley. It is difficult to find the words to express adequately my love and gratitude for your support. No matter what I ask of you, you give so generously. When I needed to make a difficult decision you stood with me in total agreement and even though you were hurting just as much as I was, you never failed to show your love and support. Your quiet strength is always a great source of comfort to me.

—*Ken Turner*

Chapter 1

My Little Girl

It was mid-morning on a cold Sunday in June. Sleeping fitfully, I became aware of an urgent voice attempting to rouse me into consciousness. The urgent voice persisted, pleading now, 'Ken! Please wake up.' I felt my wife's gentle hands shaking me. Was I dreaming? I wasn't sure.

Chronic Fatigue Syndrome had plagued me for several years, but this was the worst attack I'd suffered for many months. Stronger medication hadn't helped and the doctor ordered me to bed. I was in no condition to argue. I couldn't handle the side-effects of the medication. I felt groggy, disoriented and out of control. During this attack, however, medication was all but forced down my throat every four hours.

'Come on, Ken. You must wake up.' There was a real urgency in Merrilyn's voice. I wasn't dreaming. Her voice sounded almost frantic. I tried to rouse myself but found it difficult to focus on what she was saying. 'Please, listen. I've just had a call from the police. It's about Shirree. Something's wrong. I think something terrible has happened to her.'

I struggled to sit up. 'What do you mean, something terrible has happened?' My head was pounding and my voice sounded thick to my own ears. Damn the medication.

'The police are on the way over to see you. It's about Shirree.'

'Merrilyn, slow down,' I said, more alert now. Her exasperated tone finally caught my attention. Had Shirree been involved in an accident? Had she been arrested? No! God, no, I thought as I struggled to get out of bed.

While I showered and dressed Merrilyn filled me in on what had happened. 'Brad called earlier,' she explained. 'He's concerned about her as well. Shirree didn't come home last night and she said nothing to him before she left about staying out. He's worried sick about her.'

'Did he say anything else?' I was beginning to worry myself.

Merrilyn told me that when Brad called earlier he was looking for his sister. She hadn't come home the previous night and it seemed nobody knew where she was. Shirree and Brad, who shared a house, had an agreement that if there was a change of plans and one of them was not coming home they would call or get a message through to the other. This time Shirree had not called, which was very unusual.

'We didn't want to wake you before because you've been so ill. But when the police called I didn't have much choice,' Merrilyn explained, trying to hide her own concern about her stepdaughter.

'It's okay. How long ago did the police call?'

'It was only a few minutes before I woke you. About twenty minutes ago.'

While we waited for the police I tried not to think the worst but a feeling of dread descended over me. I didn't want to admit that I was very afraid for Shirree. Please, God, let this be a mistake, some horrible misunderstanding, I prayed silently, trying to suppress the mounting panic as the minutes ticked by.

No matter how hard I tried to stop my thoughts the worst kind of scenarios kept coming to me. While my imagination was running riot, creating chaos in my head, my logical mind concluded that if the police were involved then Shirree must have been in some kind of accident. But if it was a car accident wouldn't they have just turned up at the door? Why the phone call first? Why a personal visit?

I don't know how many minutes passed before Merrilyn led three detectives into the living room, fear and confusion all over her face. I could tell by the manner of the plain-clothed detectives that the reason for this visit was not anything I wanted to know about.

'Mr Turner,' the first man said, producing identification, 'I'm Detective Ken Raymond, Adelaide CIB Major Crime Division. These are Detectives Dave Boorman and Brian Kimber.' I shook hands with the detectives, glancing briefly at their identification. Major Crime Division? Why the hell would detectives from Major Crime want to talk to me about Shirree?

The detectives politely declined the seats that I offered. Their faces were grave; obviously their mission was a difficult one. Detective Raymond did most of the talking. 'I'm sorry to break into your day like this but we have a matter of some importance to talk to you about,' he said sombrely. 'Do you have a daughter named Shirree Ann Turner?'

I opened my mouth to speak but found my voice had deserted me. I nodded slowly. 'Earlier this morning, in the suburb of Marion, police were alerted when the body of a young woman was found on the front porch of a house near Oaklands Park Reserve. We believe that young woman could be Shirree.' Each word hit me like a stun grenade. I did not respond for a moment. My bewildered thoughts alternated between shock and disbelief, and a forlorn hope that this might be a bad dream.

Merrilyn's gasp of horror was followed by a groan of anguish. I was to remember later the helpless, sick feeling in my stomach as the bottom dropped out of my world. 'No!' My mind was racing. 'This cannot be happening. Shirree can't be dead. No way! I only spoke to her yesterday and she was so happy.' I tried to reason that because the detectives seemed uncertain that this unfortunate young woman was Shirree, maybe they were mistaken, but the look on their faces told me a different story.

'Mr Turner, I'm sorry but we have to ask you to accompany us to the morgue. We will need somebody to identify the body,' Detective Raymond said. 'Do you think you will be able to do that or would you like us to contact someone else to do it for you?'

As tempted as I was to have somebody else take on the responsibility I couldn't think of anyone that I could ask to perform such a task. Any number of people would have helped, but damn it, how could I ask someone else to do it for me?

I pulled on my jacket and walked over to Merrilyn who was standing near the doorway, still sobbing quietly. I held her for a few moments. 'You'd better take the kids to your parents' house,' I said gently. My stepchildren were playing in the yard at the back of the house and had no idea what was going on inside.

'What am I going to tell them?' Merrilyn asked, wiping her tears with the handkerchief I offered.

'I don't know,' I said, trying to think quickly. I must have sounded calmer than I was feeling. 'Try not to worry them. We don't know anything for sure yet. I want you to contact Brad and get him to come over and stay with you while I go with the detectives.' I looked into her panic-stricken eyes. 'Can I count on you?'

She nodded uncertainly. I knew I was asking a lot but what choice did I have? 'Merrilyn, I need to know. Can I count on you to contact Brad for me and handle things with the kids until I get back?' I said, trying to hide the rising panic in my voice. Bravely, Merrilyn stopped crying. I kissed her cheek gently, turned and nodded to the detectives. Somehow I found the strength to follow them out of the door and into the police car.

The trip to the morgue seemed to take forever. I was feeling very uncomfortable and wanted to ask questions. Detective Raymond broke the silence. 'We didn't find anything with her to give any firm idea of identity. That's the reason we need somebody who knows her well to identify her.'

'What is your gut feeling?' I asked.

'Unofficially, we believe it is Shirree,' he replied.

'Somebody has to officially identify her?'

'I'm afraid so. It's not a pleasant exercise but unavoidable under the circumstances.' Hope was fading fast. I was very afraid that my worst nightmare was about to become a reality. I was clinging stubbornly to the slim chance that somehow there had been a mistake.

We travelled the rest of the journey in silence. The police car stopped outside the morgue. It was a small-fronted brownstone building on a corner in King William Street, the main street that bisects the city of Adelaide. The detectives escorted me through the front door into a reception area. I looked around, wishing I were anywhere but here. One of the detectives pressed a button designed to alert a receptionist of our arrival. It was Sunday and there was only a skeleton staff on duty.

An attendant dressed in loose white lab trousers and a brilliant white surgical shirt approached us from the end of a long corridor. He spoke to one of the detectives and then indicated that we should follow him. I had to walk quickly to keep up. My heart was pounding so hard that I was sure the detectives could hear every beat.

Finally, the attendant turned into a room at the end of the corridor. The room was sparsely furnished, just a few chairs along one wall. There were more detectives present and I was introduced to each of them. Their sombre expressions made my heart skip a few beats. I felt like I might pass out. I had to take a few deep breaths to steady myself.

One of the detectives quietly explained what was about to occur. 'Mr Turner, when you are ready we will take you over to that window,' he said, indicating a large window in the far wall. 'Behind the glass is a stainless steel gurney. The body will be covered with a white sheet. An attendant will fold the sheet back from her face but only her head will be shown to you.'

I nodded, not trusting my voice. I now realised that I was expected to confirm what they somehow already knew. I prayed silently as the knots in my stomach tightened. Please God, not Shirree. Please don't let this be my daughter. I walked slowly towards the window and held my breath as the curtain opened and the sheet was drawn back revealing the face of the victim.

Chapter 2

Tears of Distress

Life changed irrevocably for me in that one brief, yet interminably long moment. I had to force myself to look at her, unwilling, yet knowing that I must. 'Oh my darling, look what they've done to you.' I bowed my head against the cold glass window. I noticed she still had make-up on. Her long wavy blonde hair circled her pretty face but her hazel eyes were closed. I wanted to hold her, to tell her that everything was going to be okay. But it wasn't okay; it was never again going to be okay. I could do nothing more than gaze at her through despairing tears.

My eyes were riveted to her lovely face. It would have been so easy to fool myself into believing that she was just asleep. She looked just as she did when she was a little girl when I used to check on her and her brother before I went to bed. I'd tuck them in and place a gentle kiss on their foreheads.

A detective disturbed my reflections. Reluctantly, I confirmed the young woman lying on the cold steel gurney was my daughter Shirree.

An almost imperceptible nod from the detective to the morgue attendant indicated the body had been officially identified and the sheet was drawn over her face.

I stood there watching, frozen to the spot, while Shirree's lifeless body was wheeled away and the curtain closed. I was led to a chair. I sat with my head in my hands and tried to gather my thoughts. The incredible distress I felt was intermingled with a myriad of questions I wanted to ask. How could this have happened to Shirree?

I felt like I was dying inside. It was a hopeless, unreal feeling. I just couldn't think of my daughter as dead. I was still thinking of the vibrant, loving girl who was such a delight to me. I wanted to go to her just as I did when she was a child and tell her that everything was going to be okay. But that wasn't possible. Never again would I be able to hold her or wipe away her tears. Never again.

Eventually I raised my head and saw that the detectives were gathered in a group, talking quietly on the opposite side of the room. One of them noticed me staring and walked over. He placed his hand on my shoulder, a gesture of surprisingly gentle comfort from such a big man. 'Are you okay, Ken? Would you like some water or something?' I shook my head.

'Are you sure you're okay?' he probed. It was a ridiculous question. I wasn't sure that I would ever be okay again but I nodded anyway. I didn't know what else to do. I was full of questions but didn't know how to ask them. They needed to know certain details about Shirree.

When the police had visited that morning they told me that the body they had found was a victim of murder. Until now I had not been thinking of anything else but the fact that my daughter was dead. I was in denial about the fact it was a murder. But the reality of the situation was beginning to penetrate. The questions in my head kept coming, adding to my uncertainty. How would life ever be the same again? How was I supposed to deal with something like this?

I remember thinking on the way to the morgue that if it had to be Shirree then I wanted it to be an accident. Murder was not a word I wanted to deal with. As I indicated that I was ready to talk with the detectives I had a moment of realisation. The nightmare was about to be lifted to another level. 'Mr Turner, I know this will be very difficult for you but we're going to need you to help us. We'd like to ask a few questions if you're up to it.' The request sounded almost apologetic.

'If I'm up to it?' I sighed heavily. I was bracing myself for what I knew would be difficult, yet necessary. 'What do you want to know?'

The police wanted personal details about Shirree and wanted to know if I knew about her plans for the previous evening. I wasn't, so I couldn't help them in that area. I gave the names of family, close friends and acquaintances that came to mind.

'We appreciate your cooperation, Ken,' one of the detectives said. 'We know how difficult it must be for you at this time.' For a moment I thought they were worried that I might not want to talk to them. Were they concerned that I might crack under the stress? Did they think I was involved in some way? I wanted them to understand how desperately I wanted to help. I realised that I could not fall in a heap. I needed the police just as much as they needed me and I had every intention of doing all I could to assist them to find Shirree's killer.

'Shirree's murder has been declared a major crime,' Detective Raymond continued, 'which means there will be a lot of media attention. Media focus will probably be quite intense initially. You should be prepared.' It was going to be humiliating having our lives displayed in the media but the police told me that they played an important role in every murder case.

A police officer handed me a plastic bag containing the hair comb and jewellery that Shirree was wearing when she was found. 'I want to know how she died,' I demanded abruptly, looking Detective Raymond squarely in the eyes.

'She was stabbed,' the detective reluctantly told me, 'and there's a strong possibility she was sexually assaulted.' I sucked in my breath and closed my eyes against this fresh horror, disgust turning to a terrified despair. There was a crushing weight in those words. 'Your daughter was stabbed to death.' What made it worse was the inference that she might have been raped. Those words invoked an intense emotion. I felt a helplessness and fear that I had never felt before and knew I would never forget.

I thought about Brad. What was I going to say to him? How could I tell him about this? How would I find the right words? What about family and friends, and Shirree's friends? How was I supposed to break this kind of news to any of them?

The drive home seemed to take a very long time. I felt as if I was the central character in some kind of horrible movie. As reluctant as I was to accept Shirree's murder I also knew that I had no choice and would have to deal with it. But how does one begin to deal with something like murder? Especially the murder of one of your children?

Several hours ago I was fighting a debilitating illness. Now I was sitting in the back seat of a police vehicle after having identified the body of my murdered daughter. All the way home I tried to find a way to break the terrible news to my son.

'You're not going to be able to soften the impact of her death for any-one no matter how hard you try,' I was told. 'They will all have to handle it in their own way, just as you will.'

The detectives discussed the probability of heavy media involvement again. They made it obvious that the media would be needed to help find Shirree's killer. The story would make front-page news. Our lives were about to be invaded by cameras and reporters and we would need to be prepared for the intrusion. But at least giving interviews to the media would give me a chance on behalf of the family to make a plea for the killer to give himself up. I could only hope that if I cooperated, the authorities would treat me with the same respect.

I also had questions the police would not answer. Always, certain details were held back to test the accuracy of information coming in. 'Please don't be offended when we seem vague or just unwilling to answer some of your questions, Ken. There is certain information that would only be known by Shirree's killer so we can't divulge some things to anyone initially, not even you.' The reality of the situation was beginning to sink in. I shook my head in disbelief yet again.

As the car inched closer to home and familiar streets passed by, commonsense began to take over. I had already decided to try to be as strong as I could. Whatever it took for her killer to be arrested quickly was my first priority, even at the expense of my own wellbeing. Though I'd hardly had time to absorb what had happened to Shirree I wanted to know everything the police knew. I had to get that idea across to them somehow.

I also had a compassionate desire to help my family deal with Shirree's death. I knew Shirree's murder would be just as devastating to our family and her many friends as it was to me. I had always tried to face my responsibilities in the past but I never had to take on anything even remotely like this before. It was not only a test of my strength of character; it was a test of my faith.

When I arrived home with the police the expression on Merrilyn's face was tragic. She could tell immediately that the news was the worst possible. I understood that she did not know what to say to me. What could she say? What could anyone say?

I glimpsed movement behind Merrilyn and saw my son standing in the doorway. The stunned look on Brad's face was heartbreaking. I had never seen, and hoped to never see again, my son look so devastated. I'd been wondering how I was going to tell him that his much-loved sister was dead. In the end, I didn't have to say a word—Brad just knew.

I reached for my son and we hugged each other tightly. Brad's emotions were alternating between great anguish and a terrifying anger. 'Why, Dad? Who would want to do this to Shirree?'

'I wish I knew, son.' I felt my response was inadequate but there was no easy way for me to answer the question. We did not say much to one another for a long time. Each time we tried, tears flowed.

I introduced Brad to the detectives who were waiting in the background. Brad told the police that the last time he'd seen Shirree was the previous evening. She was excited about going out with her girlfriends, Kirsty and Sonia.

Detective Raymond took Brad's details and made tentative plans to meet with him later that day. The police wanted to check out Shirree's bedroom and collect photographs and diaries, anything that might be useful to the investigation. 'I know that this is going to be difficult for you, Brad, but we're going to need your help as well. Anything you think of, it doesn't matter how insignificant it might seem, could be helpful. If you come up with anything that might assist us we would appreciate if you called immediately. I cannot stress enough the importance of getting information to us as soon as possible. We'll leave contact details before we go for you and your father. Please do not hesitate to call us, day or night.'

It occurred to me suddenly and with such impact that I couldn't believe that I hadn't thought of it earlier. 'Shirree's mother! Has anybody told Christine yet?' Another wave of panic washed over me.

Detective Raymond looked up from his notebook. 'We'll do that for you, Ken,' he said reassuringly. 'I'll need some contact details. You know, a phone number and address.'

The police finished interviewing us and left the house. I presumed they would head directly to Christine's house. I needed to begin the calls to relatives and friends. I wanted to be the one to tell the closest family members and Shirree's friends. But I was still putting off making the calls.

I began to wonder how much more I was going to be able to take. It had only been a few hours since I'd identified Shirree's body and I desperately needed a break. I just needed thirty minutes alone to try and absorb some of what was going on inside my head. I needed to think without being distracted. No phones—nothing. The adrenaline coursing though my veins had kept me from collapsing so far but how much longer could I rely on that? I still had so much to do and so much to think about.

The pressure of making the phone calls weighed heavily on me but I needed to find out what Brad knew about the previous evening. Brad's voice was shaking as he spoke. 'Shirree, Kirsty and Sonia planned this night some time ago. They all have birthdays next month and last night was the only night they could go out together to celebrate. You know, Dad, typical girls' night out. They went to the usual places down Hindley Street, I guess.'

'Sonia called me about eight-thirty this morning. Apparently Shirree became separated from them. I think they were at the Charles Sturt Tavern at the time. They looked for her for a while and couldn't find her so they decided to go home. The trouble was that Shirree had their handbags with her.' Brad was becoming upset again.

'Take it easy, Brad.' I encouraged him to continue, 'Just tell me what you know.'

'Kirsty and Sonia came around to the house. I checked Shirree's bedroom. She wasn't there and her bed hadn't been slept in. Dad, she always let me know if she wasn't coming home. I knew something was wrong. We called Evan to find out if she was with him.'

Shirree and Evan had only been seeing each other for a few months. They started going out shortly after a messy break-up with Fabio, her previous boyfriend. Brad continued, 'Sonia said that Evan had told Shirree to call his mobile phone when she was ready to go home and he would come and pick them up.'

'What did Evan say?'

'We didn't speak to Evan. His mother answered the phone and she told us Shirree wasn't there. He was asleep when Kirsty called. She woke him and he told her he hadn't heard from Shirree. He didn't know where she was.'

Evan was a taxi driver and worked the night shift every Saturday night. Saturday night through to 5 am Sunday morning was the busiest time of the week for taxi drivers.

'After Kirsty and Sonia left I couldn't go back to sleep. I turned on the radio and heard about the murder on the news. That's when I called Merrilyn the first time. Then I got a call from Darlington Police. They said Shirree's handbag had been handed in and they were holding it at the police department.'

The call had really disturbed Brad, who was already apprehensive about Shirree's disappearance. 'The cops said that a passing motorist found three handbags on Marion Road and driver's licences and other papers led them to call. I told them Shirree hadn't come home but I'd let her know about her handbag when she did. Then I said I would contact Kirsty and Sonia and tell them their handbags were at Darlington. I got really worried after the cops called. That's when I called Merrilyn the second time.' Brad was too upset to continue.

'So that's how the police knew it was Shirree,' I said shakily.

'What do you mean, Dad?'

'When the police came here earlier to tell me that they thought Shirree was the victim I got the distinct impression they knew it was Shirree even though there was no identification with her. When you told them you'd seen Sonia and Kirsty earlier and that you would let them know where their handbags were, they put two and two together. Shirree hadn't come home and none of you knew where she was. I guess it doesn't take a genius to figure it out.'

I couldn't put it off any longer. I could see that Brad was too upset to go on and didn't have anything more to say. I picked up the phone and dialed my mother's number. 'Mum, I want you to sit down. I have some terrible news ...'

My mother was a strong woman. In fact her strength in adversity amazed me. When I told her what had happened to Shirree, as upset as she was, she simply said, 'I'm coming over.' She should never have had to deal with this kind of tragedy again. She had been widowed suddenly in her mid-thirties and had to raise three teenagers on her own. She'd returned to work after my father's death and had done it tough trying to make ends meet. She didn't need this. None of my family were demonstrative people but in times of trouble they rallied around one another and it was no different this time.

Each time I picked up the phone to make a call I could feel a little more strength drain away from me. Physically and emotionally I was running on empty. I was exhausted and wanted to crawl back into bed but I knew I would not be able to sleep. I needed time to sort out my feelings.

I had been assured that Shirree's identity would not be released until later the next afternoon. In the meantime, we tried to contact as many relatives and friends as we could. Each call became a little more difficult. Shirree's friends were shattered. They could not believe the shocking news. We had relatives living in other states and had trouble reaching some of them. Reactions were different. Some dissolved into tears immediately while others stoically offered to help if needed.

I told the family that the media representatives would want to speak with us and it soon became another looming issue. I wondered how long it would be before they contacted me. After more phone calls I took a little time to re-energise but it was impossible to switch off completely, so I stopped trying. Merrilyn answered the doorbell. My mother and sister Kathy had arrived. I embraced them both, grateful that they had dropped everything to come. I needed them.

Early in the evening, after friends and family had left, I realised one of Shirree's closest friends had not been told of her death. Fabio was Shirree's ex-boyfriend but they remained very good friends. They had been an item for around five years. Shirree met Fabio when she worked as a receptionist for a car dealer where Fabio was a mechanic. Just before they broke up, Shirree and Fabio were planning to announce their engagement. Even though they had gone through a rocky period immediately after the break-up, they still remained close. Although I had disapproved of the way Fabio treated Shirree sometimes, I genuinely liked him. I knew I had to call him.

'Fabio. It's Ken Turner.'

'Hi, Ken.' He sounded puzzled. 'What can I do for you?'

'I have some bad news, I'm sorry to say. I don't quite know how to tell you this but ...' I had to stop talking for a moment. I swallowed the lump in my throat and continued, '... Shirree is dead ... sometime early this morning ... she was murdered.' My voice was breaking up.

There was a brief silence. Fabio spoke, obviously distressed. 'Shit! How? What ... do you know what happened?'

'She was stabbed.'

'Shit. No! I can't believe it. What happened? How the hell ...'

'Look, I can't talk about this right now. I just wanted to let you know before you hear it from somebody else. Will you be okay?'

'I don't know what to say. I can't believe it ... I spoke to her a couple of days ago.' Fabio was distraught. 'Shit! Ken ... you must be wiped out. I can't talk any more. I'll call you tomorrow.'

'Sure,' I said, still feeling the aftershocks of the day.

I replaced the phone, relieved the call was over. I had dreaded talking to Fabio because I had my suspicions that Fabio was still in love with Shirree. Fabio had not been happy about the way the relationship ended. Shirree decided to end it after much thought and indecision. Fabio was too possessive. He disapproved of some of the places Shirree liked to go when she went out and it was getting on her nerves. He'd become hot-headed occasionally and lost his temper several times. It was mostly verbal abuse. Shirree told Fabio that she was sick of his attitude and they'd had a few nasty exchanges during the last few weeks of the relationship.

Even so, the past six months had seen a marked change in Fabio's attitude. He and Shirree had formed an easygoing friendship. I suspected that although Shirree had moved on and was seeing another man, Fabio secretly harboured the hope they might get back together in the future.

Shirree had confided in me about the relationship. I knew that she was unhappy about breaking up with Fabio; I was also aware that Shirree thought the relationship had been serious. Serious enough to be dreaming of a future with Fabio. She was really happy about the new friendship they had developed despite their previous history.

I needed time alone to think, to rest and try to come to terms with what was happening. I watched the news on television. An extensive report on the murder was shown and video footage from the crime scene covered the screen for several minutes.

Merrilyn left to bring the children home and I found myself alone for the first time that day. I leaned my head back against the chair and closed my eyes. My head ached and I couldn't turn my thoughts off. I was exhausted, yet I couldn't sit still for long. I paced around for a while, trying to settle down, not knowing what to do with myself.

Memories of Shirree and our relationship flooded back in waves. It was like a picture show. I remembered things I thought I'd forgotten; things that were as fresh as the day they occurred. Like the day my beautiful girl was born, her first real smile, her first steps, the way she reacted to her little brother when we brought him home from hospital. I remembered when she returned from her first day at school and when she introduced her first best friend to us. I remembered the first tooth she lost and how she thought her whole world had come to end until we reassured her that she would grow a new tooth that would be even stronger than the last one. I was so completely overwhelmed by these memories that I collapsed into my favourite chair and sobbed uncontrollably, releasing my grief and despair in a flood of tears.

When Merrilyn arrived home with the children I sat them down and explained how sad I was and told them why. I was amazed at their reaction, but uncertain that they fully understood the implications of what I told them. Even though there were tears, they were sort of happy that heaven now had an extra angel to watch over them. Davina, who was seven at the time, and Gary, who was five, were too young to really deal with Shirree's death. Merrilyn and I decided that we wouldn't hide what happened to Shirree because they were both at school and we wanted them to hear the truth from us first.

Shirree's love for children had been extended to her new stepsister and stepbrother and they loved her, too. They were going to miss her. Merrilyn put the children to bed and once again I tried to close my eyes and rest. I knew I wasn't going to be able to sleep so I just leaned back in my chair and let my thoughts drift. I hoped I might be able to sleep for a couple of hours at least. I was utterly exhausted.

It wasn't long before the phone interrupted my thoughts. It was nearly 7 pm and although completely wiped out and not wanting to answer the call, I picked up the receiver in case it was the police. 'Hi, Mr Turner, it's Evan. I've been unable to contact Shirree and I wondered if she might be at your house.'

I shuddered. 'Evan, you had better come over here as soon as you can. I have something I need to talk to you about.'

I had no idea what Evan must have thought, but when he arrived a short time later I told him as gently as I knew how that Shirree had been murdered. I didn't know what to expect and was completely caught off guard by Evan's reaction. Tears of distress tumbled down his face.

After Evan had calmed down we talked for about two hours. I was relieved when he left. I hadn't known Evan for as long as I'd known Fabio and felt uncomfortable talking to him under the circumstances. Confronting the two men who were closest to Shirree, after Brad and myself, with news of her death was almost as stressful as telling my family.

Once again I closed my eyes. My mind drifted to the day Shirree was born. Our new little baby was totally dependent. I was astounded how quickly Christine adapted to motherhood and the calm confidence she displayed when handling our first child. The excitement and love that I felt when I saw mother and tiny daughter interacting overwhelmed me. Christine seemed to know instinctively what to do. She was so in tune with what Shirree needed and when she needed it. By contrast, I felt so inadequate and clumsy, even when holding our baby girl. 'She won't break,' Christine laughed as I gazed at her tiny hands and feet, completely in awe, feeling paternal and so proud to be her father.

In the end I took Christine's word for it and began to relax a little. Shirree opened her eyes and seemed to focus on me. Her forehead creased into a tiny frown. I knew that her eyes were not seeing clearly yet but they were the prettiest eyes I had ever seen. Christine smiled; we were both feeling the same and counted our blessings that Shirree Ann had come into the world, perfect in every way.

The birth of a child is a special milestone in a parent's life. There is a deeper understanding of love, a broader perspective on life itself and a shared bond that simply doesn't compare to anything else. Chris and I had big dreams. We loved the idea of family. What the hell had gone wrong? Where had the dream gone?

I was jolted back from my memories to the reality of the day's events. My former sister-in-law had phoned to let me know that Christine had collapsed at the news of Shirree's murder and been taken to hospital. Again, I dissolved into a flood of tears. Merrilyn did her best to console me but she was trying to handle her own grief, torn between her concern for me and trying to answer the children's questions.

'I think the only way the kids are going to settle down is if I sleep in the room with them,' she said.

'You go to the kids,' I told her. 'It's more important that you tend to them. I'll be okay.' It was becoming my catchcry.

After the phone call about Christine's admission to hospital I managed to drift off to sleep for a short time. Merrilyn placed a blanket over me but I woke feeling very cold. As soon as I was conscious, my mind cranked up again. I rose from the chair, wrapped the blanket around myself and stumbled into the kitchen to make a cup of tea.

While I waited for the kettle to boil the 'why' questions came. Why would somebody want to kill Shirree? Why did she and her friends go to the Hindley Street nightclub strip? I'd often told Shirree of my fears about her going to nightclubs but she always felt that I was being over-protective. 'It's okay, Dad,' she'd told me on a number of occasions. 'I know heaps of people there. We all look out for each other.'

I wasn't convinced. 'There must be safer venues to go out and have fun,' I'd complained. I thought about what the police and Brad had told me about Shirree's movements on the night she was killed and I began to build a picture in my mind of what might have happened. But how did she meet with her attacker? Did she know him? The questions continued to haunt me. The police indicated she might very well have known her killer. They came to that conclusion because there appeared to be no real signs of a struggle leading into the reserve.

The evidence suggested that Shirree was probably taken to the reserve by car, but there was no access for a vehicle into the reserve. She must have been led down a short lane to the spot where she was assaulted and after her attacker fled she must have stumbled and crawled eighty metres to the house where she died on the porch.

But Shirree would never have gone willingly with someone she didn't know. The more I thought about it, the more questions arose. Who would she know that might be capable of murder? And why would anybody who knew her attack her so viciously? It really bothered me that one of the men Shirree knew might have killed her. But who?

I thought about her male friends. None seemed the type to commit murder. I considered Evan and Fabio. They were probably the most obvious. Could one of them have killed her? I didn't like to think so. Evan had been very upset when I told him about Shirree's murder, but could he have been faking it?

Fabio was also very distraught when I phoned him. Could that have been an act? I couldn't believe either of them would be so callous. As hot-headed and verbally abusive as Fabio might have been at times, I just couldn't believe he would risk the wrath of his family. They loved Shirree and would never have tolerated any physical violence toward her. I could not believe Fabio would hurt her physically, no matter how angry he got.

Fabio's family had all but adopted Shirree and his mother was like a substitute mother. Lina taught Shirree to cook Fabio's favourite Italian dishes and treated her as if she were a member of the family. Shirree fitted in very well and even took classes to learn the Italian language, so she could understand and communicate with them when they got together for large family gatherings.

I had no doubt that Fabio loved Shirree. In her diaries Shirree expressed a desire to marry and have a family, hoping Fabio would be the one who would share her life. But in the end, she couldn't cope with his verbal outbursts and domineering attitude. The split between them, although rocky in the beginning, became amicable and I believed Fabio held the hope that Shirree would get over her infatuation with Evan and come back to him.

I didn't know Evan well, but what I knew did not point to his being capable of murder. At least I didn't want to think so. I checked my watch. It was 3 am I wanted to try to get more sleep. I was still very cold and even burying myself under the covers could not warm me. Each time I closed my eyes I saw Shirree. Memories of special times with my daughter invaded my thoughts.

There was nothing outstanding or extraordinary about Shirree, except in my eyes. To me she was very special, my little girl, my princess, my pride and joy. She was like every other young adult trying to find her own way, finally free from the constraints of parents and looking forward to fulfilling her dreams and desires.

To her friends she was loyal, friendly, loving and she could be counted on. She worked part-time as a childcare worker. Kids were special to Shirree and she gravitated toward them like a magnet to steel. She was naturally gifted in taking care of children.

I thought about her wonderful sense of humour. She had the gift of laughter, which made everyone around her want to laugh, too. I remembered a time when I came home from work and found the loungeroom furniture completely rearranged. It looked like a disaster area and

Shirree cracked up laughing at my reaction. She said she was bored with how the room looked and had decided to change it. I was not impressed, but instead of being hurt by my reaction she thought it was hilarious. I was never quite sure if she thought I was old-fashioned or if she knew what my reaction would be and was testing to me to see if she was right.

Shirree loved a practical joke and would dissolve into gales of laughter after acting out a joke on an unsuspecting recipient. She and Fabio loved to play around with the video camera. They were always filming their friends, family and anything else that took their fancy. They would play around and make people disappear and reappear in entirely ridiculous ways and make smart comments about what they were doing. We had some special evenings laughing about their film-making efforts 'starring' unsuspecting family and friends. Her sense of fun was incorrigible.

She was generous, held in high esteem by her friends and could be trusted implicitly. Even if her personal life was tumultuous, she always made time for family. I always felt an immense sense of pride when I thought about her. I had every reason to be proud of her. She had grown into a lovely young woman.

Shirree was blissfully unaware of the dangers of the Hindley Street environment. She was convinced that she could handle herself in any circumstances and in most cases she could. I had always tried to understand her choices, loving her despite my fatherly fears. Her beautiful hazel eyes would flash such confidence in her ability to look after herself but it was not enough to convince me and I had continued to worry about her. She wasn't afraid to take a risk and her friendliness and naivete probably led to her death.

Why? And more to the point, who? And where were the people who she was convinced she could depend on that night? The ones who looked out for each other?

Chapter 3
A Public Goodbye

Giving up on getting any useful rest I showered and dressed, reluctant to greet the new day. The morning paper covered the murder under the headline, 'Murder link to city clubs'.[1] Scanning the page I found Shirree's identity had not been released but an extensive article covered most of the known facts. The article described the murder as 'brutal'. I shuddered as I read about the bloodstained trail left as she staggered from where she was attacked to the front porch of the house where she collapsed and died from multiple stab wounds to her chest.

My eyes filled with tears as a fresh wave of sadness engulfed me. 'Oh! Shirree, how could this have happened to you?' The article went on to say that her murder was the third stabbing murder in Adelaide in five weeks. Detectives were seconded from the Organised Crime Task Force to investigate Shirree's murder because the Major Crime Unit was so busy.

I began to wonder how many other families out there had experienced something similar. How did other families cope with the murder of loved ones? I had been given information about the Victims of Crime Support Group but I was not ready to contact them. I couldn't deal with anyone probing into my situation yet and had other, more pressing priorities.

The first newspaper story stated that the identity of the victim would be released later in the day. The media circus was about to begin in earnest and I wondered how long it would be before they were camped on my doorstep.

In an effort to shield my family I chose to speak to the media myself. From late that morning to mid-afternoon I was busy. Still battling exhaustion I bravely faced reporters and cameras, pleading with the killer to have some compassion and give himself up to the authorities.

I agreed to an interview with a journalist from *The Advertiser* that would concentrate more on Shirree, the woman. The journalist made it easy to talk about the daughter I loved and had lost in such a brutal fashion. We strolled through Shirree's life with the aid of family photo albums. A picture of a delightful, bright and bubbly youngster began to emerge. We tracked her growth into a young woman. I remembered a video made of Shirree's twenty-first birthday, which gave further insight into a young life so full of potential.

After the interview I felt like I had to get out of the house. The police suggested that if I wanted to visit the murder site I should contact them. I was worried about Brad, who had also decided to visit the scene of the murder. Evan went with him. I didn't think it was a good idea but they wanted to visit the place where Shirree died. I called and arranged to meet a detective at the site.

I wandered in a daze around the area where Shirree had been attacked, then retraced the path she took to the house where she had collapsed and died. Both areas were cordoned off with yellow tape. The trail of blood had been sprayed with a substance that preserved and highlighted its path from the reserve. I was not permitted to go close to the porch. I stood for a long time on the footpath staring at the painted outline of

Shirree's body. Detectives were still searching for clues, combing the surrounding area for forensic evidence. Rubbish bins and bushes around the reserve were thoroughly searched but no weapon was found. The police extensively door-knocked the area, gaining very little information.

Shirree had left blood-stained handprints on the brick wall just below the doorbell. My gaze shifted to the handprints. It was obvious she made every effort to get help. The sick, helpless feeling had returned and although the images I was seeing would have a lasting effect on me, I felt that if I had not visited the scene I would have regretted it for the rest of my life.

The police had appointed a liaison officer to keep me informed about the progress of the investigation. The officer had called to introduce himself and update us. The officer assured us he would answer our questions if he could, but warned us that he could not disclose sensitive information until Detective Johnson gave the okay. Johnson was in charge and the liaison officer took his cues from his boss. 'I understand your frustration and the fact that you will have many questions. I can promise I will do all I can to keep you fully informed about the status of the case.'

There'd been little headway. Although the investigation was still in its embryonic stage I was surprised to hear many calls had been received. The police were hopeful that once the media could report more of the story, except for the sensitive information, other sightings would confirm those already received. This would give a more accurate picture of Shirree's movements in the hours leading up to her death. The police were counting on the fact that an attractive woman carrying more than one handbag, and possibly a camera, would attract more than a cursory glance from people who were in the Hindley Street and Rundle Mall area between 1 am and 3 am on the night she was murdered.

Kirsty and Sonia were interviewed extensively. They had been planning an evening out for some time to celebrate their joint birthdays. They met at Kirsty's apartment, opened some champagne and started their birthday celebrations early in the evening. They were driven downtown later that night and visited several well-known nightspots before ending up at the Charles Sturt Tavern around midnight. The Tavern was not as crowded as the other venues they had been to. One of their favourite songs was playing and Kirsty and Sonia headed for the dance floor. Shirree was talking with a man at the bar and declined the invitation to dance with them, so the girls asked Shirree to look after their handbags.

When the girls returned to the bar, Shirree was nowhere to be found. They searched the Tavern and, not finding her, went outside to see if she had gone for some fresh air. Still unable to find her they decided to go home since they didn't have any money; Shirree had their handbags. It was about 1 am at this point.

The best scenario police could hope for was that somebody had seen her with the man who attacked her and a good description would be made available, ensuring a quick arrest. I returned calls from relatives and friends before watching the television news. I watched myself tell a reporter, 'I can forgive the man but I hate what he has done to Shirree. She was a loving, trusting girl and needed people around her, she was always disappointed that people would want to hurt each other.'

The tears, constantly near the surface, tumbled down my face as I watched the report. The body of my daughter was placed in a dark blue body bag and removed from the porch on a gurney. I then saw it pushed roughly into the coroner's ambulance. The imprint of two bloodied handprints on the brick wall could be clearly seen. While these graphic visions were shown the presenter related details of the crime. The focus of the investigation now centred on a one-hour window of time between 3 am and 4 am.

Police made a strong appeal for information from the public and a Crime Line number was flashed onto the screen. Another report detailed some of the places Shirree was reported to have been seen. There'd been information from witnesses who claimed to have seen a woman carrying three handbags at various times and places in Hindley Street and Rundle Mall. The significance of the three handbags would be a telling factor for the police in tracing Shirree's last movements.

A terrible sadness descended over me again. My emotions were fluctuating. I knew nothing could bring Shirree back. I felt I was beginning to accept it but then sadness would strike again. My conscious mind knew that I needed to grieve but I also felt compelled to put on a brave face in public.

I had experienced grief only once before. I was fifteen when my father died of massive heart failure during a football game. The doctors had warned my father that he could no longer play the sport he dearly loved. They said that his heart could not cope with strenuous activity and he was forced to retire from his beloved Aussie Rules.

However, he had not been able to stay away from the game for long. My father took up coaching with the same enthusiasm as he played. And he was a very good coach. The day he died his team was one player short. My father made a fatal decision. He filled in to give the team the best chance to win. It was only supposed to be for that one game but his heart couldn't stand it. He collapsed and died on the field.

My brother, sister, mother and I were devastated. I had grieved for the loss of my father as a teenager, but this was entirely different. I still anticipated Shirree walking through the door at any moment. There was still an expectation when the phone rang that I would pick up the receiver and hear her voice. 'Hi Dad! I just wanted to check you were home. I'm coming over so don't you go out anywhere.' I would never again hear her voice saying those or any other words again. The pain that came with each realisation was indescribable.

To date I had shown little visible pain although it felt like I had descended to the bottom of an immense black hole. I had to learn how to climb out one step at a time and sometimes it felt like I was doing it alone. I didn't want to burden the people around me who were feeling similar emotions.

I was too afraid to sleep. Each time I closed my eyes I saw Shirree. I couldn't help but reflect on special moments, celebrations and father–daughter talks. Even hard times had special meaning. I kept having random memories of Shirree's life flicker through my mind.

After we had divorced, Christine was granted custody of both of our children. However, Shirree came to live with me about three months later. 'I can't stay with Mum any more,' she cried. At an age when she needed a mother's constant attention, she couldn't cope with Christine's bouts of illness. Brad missed his sister so much that he also chose to come back to live with me. Both children refused to return to their mother and I was reluctant to force the issue. I felt they'd dealt with enough emotional trauma and I was more than willing to take the role of a single parent. It wasn't an easy time. Shirree needed a mother in whom she could confide.

When Shirree was fourteen she was very confused about what was happening to her and didn't feel like she had her mother's support, as Christine was again very sick. Although I tried, I just couldn't seem to get through to Shirree. She decided she wanted to live with some friends and left home.

I was frantic. She hadn't contacted me for some time and I didn't know where she was. I remember standing out in the car yard where I worked as a Fleet Car Sales Manager when our receptionist announced over the PA system that I had a call. It was Shirree; I remember the joy I felt hearing her voice. She wanted me to know that she was okay and that she loved me. They were the sweetest words I had heard for a long time. Not long after that she returned home.

I felt a profound sadness, as all of Shirree's unfulfilled plans became my shattered dreams. I would never have the honour of walking my only daughter down the aisle on her wedding day or the privilege of welcoming Shirree's choice of a partner into our family. Nor would I ever feel the joy of having grandchildren from this union. She would have been a wonderful mother—but some evil faceless bastard had destroyed the dream for both of us.

I was also worried about Brad. He and Shirree were best friends, always backing each other up, and I had to remember that he was hurting, too. My concerns about Brad centred on my own early interactions with the media. Brad, although fully supportive of the police investigation and media involvement and willing to help in any way he could, preferred to remain in the background, maintaining a very low profile. He felt that he couldn't cope with the media attention and was comforted by the fact that I was more than prepared to deal with the media on behalf of the whole family.

Brad was developing a deep-seated anger and hatred for Shirree's killer and this realisation frightened me. He had been known to lose his cool in the past trying to protect his sister, and was finding it extremely difficult to deal with the fact that the police felt Shirree's killer might have been known to her. If that was indeed true, then it was highly likely that Brad would know him also and he couldn't help but ponder who he might be and why somebody who might know her could treat her in such a brutal fashion. I knew exactly how he felt.

I was having enough difficulty dealing with my own grief and the seemingly endless questions from the police and the media wanting to know more and more about Shirree and the status of the case. Then there was family and friends who also wanted to be kept informed. While all of this was going on, Brad was trying to deal with his own grief, so I purposefully planned that I would take most of the heat from the media.

While I was protective of Brad, he was trying to put on a brave face so that I didn't need to worry about him and so I could concentrate on what I needed to be doing. It didn't stop the emotions he was feeling over his sister's murder from boiling around inside him. I knew that my mother was a tower of strength for Brad and she was giving him all the support she could. That knowledge gave me the freedom to do what I had to do.

Brad and I had long and quite emotional talks. It was a volatile situation for him and he feared that his reactions to personal questions might not be appropriate in the media. I kept him fully updated at all times in an attempt to help him to deal with his feelings. I was reminded of times when Shirree and Brad were young. When somebody picked on Shirree for any reason, Brad was always there to defend her and although they had their own brother and sister spats they interacted with each other very well. They enjoyed being together, hatching plans to surprise their mother and me, even sharing friends although they had their own special friends as well. But they loved to be together and do things together.

Their special friendship made access visits such wonderful times after their mother and I divorced. We could enjoy our time together and I have treasured memories of those times. My mind replayed these memories over and over and before long I drifted off to sleep again, deciding that I would make a special photo album for Brad to keep in memory of his beloved sister.

I woke a short time later feeling terrible. The intensity of my fear scared me. I was sweating profusely, breathing very quickly, couldn't stop trembling and my heart was racing. The feeling was unlike anything I had experienced in the past. I'd had a nightmare and tried to remember what it was about, too afraid to close my eyes again. Parts of the dream were hazy but I remembered hearing Shirree screaming in terror. Stumbling in a blind panic, surrounded by her cries for help, I was trying desperately to find her. My legs became very heavy as I ran toward her. I couldn't lift my feet. It was as though I was running through thick mud. My panic intensified as I realised I was moving in slow motion and Shirree's terrified screams were fading into a distant abyss. I was running in the wrong direction. Arms outstretched, my head was turning from side to side trying to gauge where her fading cries were coming from. And then I woke up.

I began to think that maybe I could have handled things differently with Shirree. Perhaps if I had taken more time to be with her and explain more clearly my fears for her safety. If only I had tried a little harder and ignored her plea not to nag her. No matter how hard I tried to stop them, hypothetical conversations about what I could have or should have done continued in my head. I was doing it again, sinking into a victim mentality. I had to stop beating myself up.

Day three dawned and the front-page headlines read, 'Girl's murder: heartbroken father blames ... "An enemy of God." '[2] I scanned the article quickly before re-reading it at a slower pace. My personal feeling toward Shirree's attacker was featured. 'He's better off coming forward because he'll be tormented all the days of his life ... he's probably living in awesome fear of what he's done.'

I'd made a statement earlier that I'd been able to forgive Shirree's murderer, but my emotional state found me vacillating between faith in my statement and wondering if it was humanly possible to forgive a killer. I felt that if I harboured bitterness, hatred and thoughts of retaliation I was asking for trouble. By forgiving Shirree's killer I gave up the right to seek revenge but it did not mean that I could not pursue justice. Somebody had taken my daughter's life and I had every right to expect justice to be served, but the example I set for family and friends was also important.

The article went on to say that Shirree's skirt had been cut or ripped open at the front from the hemline almost to the waist and that her underwear was also cut open, giving the appearance of a sexual attack, but forensic tests had yet to determine whether rape had occurred. My horror was only compounded by the realisation that Shirree might have endured a degrading sexual attack. Her horrible death pushed this fact into the background but the description of her ripped clothing made me shake with rage. I couldn't understand what would drive a man to take advantage of a young woman in such a cowardly manner.

In the newspaper report Shirree's love of the beach, the fact that she was a keen netball player, together with some personal details about her life, profiled a young woman just beginning to emerge into her own person. It went on to say the man who found Shirree's body was having trouble coming to terms with what had happened. He said the whole neighbourhood had been affected. In fact, the entire city was feeling uncomfortable. Three stabbing murders in the space of a few weeks made everyone jittery.

My thoughts turned toward planning Shirree's funeral. The Coroner would not release her body until the autopsy report was completed but I felt it would be unwise to leave everything until the last minute. I made the decision to contact a funeral director, if not that day, then the next. I didn't want the funeral to be a rushed event.

The police finally contacted me. The Coroner had completed the autopsy and was ready to release Shirree's body. Shirree was buried ten days after the murder. It was during the period of waiting just before the funeral that I experienced my first, full-on panic attack and it left me terrified. I struggled to breathe, feeling like I was having a heart attack, a vice-like grip trying to squeeze the air out of my lungs.

I couldn't believe the rapidity of the symptoms. They manifested one after the other with frightening speed. My vision was affected, as if I'd had too much to drink or a bad reaction to some medication. My heart pounded violently, I was alternately light-headed, then feeling as if my head was so heavy it might fall from my shoulders. Dizziness followed, my head spinning wildly out of control. And while I fought the fear and panic building inside, nausea seemed to sneak up from nowhere. It was on me before I realised what was happening. The attacks became more frequent as time passed. A panic attack often accompanied a nightmare and the assault on my emotions was almost more than I could cope with. I needed help.

There were times when I retreated into myself and couldn't allow anybody close to me. These times were especially difficult for those around me who were trying their best to stand with me, yet were deep in the throes of grief themselves. I had difficulty showing my emotions and this made me seem a little remote at times. My wife, Merrilyn, was beginning to feel more and more left out of my life. She was having her own battle with grief and she had the added responsibility of two young, grieving children.

I knew that I could not go on like this. Somewhere in the back of my mind I knew the feelings were probably to be expected but I had no idea how to deal with them. I had to get professional help before I went insane. I could hardly believe I was capable of making rational decisions but something inside me decided I was not going to become a victim. 'Whatever it takes,' I told myself. 'Whatever it takes.'

I made a conscious decision to seek help. It wasn't healthy to let the pressure build and the cycle couldn't be broken until I decided to break it. It was impossible to describe what was going on inside my head or my heart. The feelings were entirely internal. 'After the funeral, that's when I'll do it, after the funeral.'

Pastor Ben Callendar officiated at the funeral service. Due to wide public interest he allowed the media into the church on condition there were no disruptions to the dignity of the service, and the media were there big time. I talked with the pastor a few days beforehand. We decided that the service should be more of a celebration of Shirree's life, rather than a sombre event. Ben wanted to bring a Christian perspective to the forefront of people's thinking. It was a good opportunity to explain that bad things happen to good people and to bring a message of hope into the hearts of the mourners who gathered to pay their respects. Ben knew Shirree and I trusted him to choose his words wisely and speak from his heart.

After discussions with most of the family I decided that prior to the service at the church we should hold a viewing of Shirree's body. She had been taken from us so abruptly that I felt a viewing might bring some closure to those who wanted to see her one more time. My mother was extremely cautious about a viewing and I was worried about how she would cope, but at the same time encouraged her to come. I strongly stressed the reasons why I felt that it would be best for each of us to say a final personal goodbye to Shirree.

The morning of the funeral was bright and sunny for a winter's day, although the atmosphere was quite cold. We arrived at the parlour as a family, meeting close friends who had decided to join us, including Evan and Fabio. I approached Shirree's coffin feeling a sense of trepidation. This would be the very last time I would see my daughter and I didn't know quite what to expect. We were given red roses to place in the casket and the first thing I noticed was how serene she looked. For a long moment I couldn't take my eyes from her hands. She had such petite hands and I felt an overwhelming sense of love for this daughter whom I would never see again, at least not on this earth. Jas, Shirree's best friend, had selected all of Shirree's favourite clothing and jewellery and given instructions to the funeral director about how make-up should be applied and what colours to use. Shirree didn't wear a lot of make-up and Jas thought she should look as natural as possible.

But it was Shirree's hands that held my attention for the first few moments. She was wearing the gold ring that I had given her for her birthday some years before on her right hand. I was fingering an opal ring that Christine had given me before we were married and still wore as a symbolic gesture signifying the bond of love that we shared for our children. Slowly I removed the ring and gently placed it on the ring finger of Shirree's left hand. The tears tumbled down my face as I bent over the casket and kissed my daughter gently on the cheek, placing my red rose carefully near her beautiful hands.

I stepped back to allow Brad to say his goodbyes. I heard him whisper,, 'How could anybody do that to Shirree?' It broke my heart to see him choking back tears, so confused and profoundly grief-stricken. Hoping to ease his pain a little I said, 'Shirree is in heaven', but I could see the struggle he was having coming to terms with his emotions.

Much of the remainder of the time in the viewing parlour passed by in a blur of emotion but I remember Fabio's reaction when he touched her hand. 'She's so cold,' he said with such sadness. Each person who filed past the coffin showed their love for Shirree and all too soon it was time to leave for the church. I indicated to the funeral director that he should close the coffin and kissed my daughter's cheek for a final time.

My mother waited for me at the entrance to the foyer of the parlour. She took my hands in hers and thanked me for talking her into viewing Shirree's body. Her face spoke a thousand words. Although profoundly saddened by what the day ahead held in terms of emotional stress, she had finally been able to accept the reality of the situation and was showing a kind of strength that I hoped I could imitate.

We travelled to the church in silence, each of us consumed with deeply private thoughts. We witnessed much love for Shirree in the form of floral tributes that were set up in the foyer of the church and outside on the footpath on several stands. Evan and Fabio, together with Shirree's cousins Adam and Jason, my brother Bob, and Les, a family friend, had consented to be bearers and carried Shirree's coffin from the hearse into the church.

Brad, Merrilyn and I followed Shirree's coffin to the front of the church and took our places in the front row. I was only just holding myself together. The church was packed with people, including relatives and friends who had travelled from Darwin, Alice Springs, Sydney and all over Adelaide to attend.

Tina, who was one of the church worship leaders, sang a song that was apparently one of Shirree's favourites. It was about crying tears that couldn't be hidden and I wasn't aware of having heard it prior to the service. The hymns had been carefully chosen to reflect hope and love for one another. I couldn't concentrate on the service, my emotions were still too raw and I was worried about Brad. He was struggling to cope and it was showing.

I was deeply humbled by the number of people who attended the church service. I was told later that many whom I hardly knew were there and the memorial book where people signed their names was a testament to the number who attended. I saw many names I didn't recognise when I looked through the signatures but I was deeply grateful to each and every one who came.

After the service, the same bearers solemnly carried the coffin from the church to the hearse again for Shirree's final journey to the Enfield Cemetery. I was too distraught to take in many of the faces who paid their condolences as we prepared to leave. A long cortege of cars followed the hearse to the cemetery and Shirree was finally laid to rest in the western rose garden, where a gathering of hundreds attended to say a final goodbye. I was physically and emotionally washed out as I watched them. Shirree's killer was still at large and stress was taking a huge toll.

Several plain-clothes police officers mingled with the several hundred mourners. I was not in any state to be aware of the significance of the police presence and Detective Johnson approached me discreetly to let me know that he and the other officers would carry out their duties with as little fuss as possible. When I became aware that Shirree's killer might have attended the funeral service I wanted to throw up. It was unthinkable that this heartless bastard could be so cruel, intruding on our grief after what he had done. My anger burned deep. 'We've viewed the video footage from the service and the cemetery,' Detective Johnson told me when I inquired. 'I'm sorry, Ken, we didn't see anything unusual or of interest to the investigation.'

The service at the gravesite was just as moving as the church service. As Shirree's coffin was lowered Christine lurched forward, tears streaming down her face in a flood of grief and emotion as her friends tried to support her. My heart went out to her; I knew just how she was feeling. Brad went to his mother to comfort her, their reunion snapped by newspaper photographers.

The morning after the funeral a very large picture covering the entire front-page of *The Advertiser* especially touched me. Lena, one of Shirree's closest friends, was photographed placing a bouquet of flowers on one of the stands outside the church. The headline read, 'Goodbye, Shirree'.[3]

The story of the funeral followed on page two. Three hundred mourners had heard Pastor Ben Callendar ask the question, 'Who is to blame? Is it society? Is it Hindley Street?' He spoke about Shirree's love and loyalty for her family and friends and how her death had affected the whole community. 'Today will be a day of very mixed emotions, sadness, grief ... and perhaps a sense of anger and senselessness,' he said. He appealed to the perpetrator to give himself up. He prayed that a sense of reality would be brought to his thinking and that justice would prevail.

Media coverage was extensive. Surely the sadness on Lena's face would tug at some heartstrings, prompting those with information to come forward. Somebody had to know something. Was it possible that at least one conscience would be sufficiently stirred to come forward—even anonymously? I visited the police to find out what, if anything, they could give me by way of a progress report. I was becoming worried because the killer's trail was getting colder by the day.

My emotional state was about to take another beating. Two weeks after Shirree's funeral Merrilyn told me she couldn't cope any longer. In my own grief and distress I had not noticed that she was also having major difficulties. I was devastated when she told me she was taking the children and leaving me.

The murder was the final straw for Merrilyn. She had been a tower of strength for the children and me since Shirree's death but how much could one person take? My attempts to talk with her were met with a stony silence. She wouldn't even talk with her pastor, the man who had married us only seven months before.

Once again I was grieving, only this time it was for the death of my marriage and the loss of the two stepchildren I had grown to love as if they were my own. This latest assault on my already fragile emotional state convinced me I could no longer go it alone. I needed more help than family and friends could give.

The Victims of Crime card had been propped against the wall behind the phone since the day of the murder. I picked up the phone and called the number. 'My name is Ken Turner. My daughter Shirree was murdered recently. I am going to need to see somebody as soon as possible. I need help.'

They were expecting my call. Most victims of crime eventually made the same call. I knew it was going to be a long, hard road but I had taken the first tentative step toward recovery. The support group appointed a social worker to my case. It was recommended that psychiatrist and counsellor, Dr Ann Williams, would be of benefit to both Brad and myself.

Brad and I were struggling to cope with Shirree's death in our own ways. I was still protecting Brad from media exposure. He still felt unable to cope with possible confrontations and was also trying to be sensitive toward the effect that the murder had on his mother. He was deliberately keeping himself in check and trying desperately to get on with his life. He had decided to go into business for himself as a contractor installing home improvements. Working by himself was easier than having to explain what had happened to his sister to workmates when the subject came up. He was becoming more of a loner and although I understood how he felt I was continually worried about his reactions in certain situations.

Brad also felt that he was out of his depth in social situations. He had become very protective towards girls and wouldn't buy them any alcoholic drinks. When the topic of Shirree's murder came up in conversation he found it very difficult to talk. It still hurt deeply, and he was not handling it at all well. Forming new relationships with anyone became almost impossible for him. He would only talk about the murder with established friends and friends of Shirree's.

After several visits to Dr Williams, Brad decided he would rather tough it out on his own but I continued to see her for several years. She helped to keep me from falling into the trap of victim mentality thinking. I had no way of controlling the images that floated through my mind. I had been trying to logically process the circumstances of Shirree's murder but my heart was undeniably broken. While my mind told me there was nothing I could do to change the circumstances my heart was crying out, how the hell was I going to deal with this? It was comforting to learn that the feelings I was experiencing were normal. I had lost a precious daughter by the evil act of murder.

During those first couple of weeks I came to expect to see reporters waiting with their cameras each time I left the house. At times I wished the media would leave me alone so I could grieve privately but it was a mutual dependence. I needed them and they needed me. I found the seemingly endless clicking of their cameras disconcerting and when television cameras were held in my face I felt even more unsettled.

I pondered the information I had heard and began to piece together a picture along similar lines to police thinking. It was like fitting pieces into a jigsaw puzzle. The clue to where each piece fitted lay in the picture on the front of the box, but neither the police nor I had the completed image to guide us.

The extent of Shirree's injuries suggested to police that she had put up a brave fight. The length of the blood-stained trail from the park to the house and the bloodied handprints on the wall near the doorbell told the tragic story that although mortally wounded Shirree must have fought very hard to hold onto her life.

Three handbags, identified as belonging to Shirree, Sonia and Kirsty, were found on Marion Road. They had been tossed from a moving car about two kilometres from where her body was found. To the police, the handbags were the clue to tracing the final hours of Shirree's life.

Day after day newspaper and television reports held appeals from the police for people to come forward. 'The information you have may not seem significant but it might be important to the investigation,' the police pleaded.

There had been several crank calls and the police were busy filtering out genuine information from false information. Crank calls were becoming part and parcel of every murder investigation.

Brad agreed to an interview for *The Advertiser*. He urged those who had information to come forward. 'Someone must have seen something. I find it difficult to understand why people won't come forward. They've got no reason to be scared. No-one will know what you tell the police,' he told the reporter.

My admiration for my son increased as the weeks continued to pass without any satisfaction coming from the police investigation. Although Brad mostly kept his thoughts very private I knew from the talks we had that he still hurt very deeply. Anniversaries were especially difficult and as time progressed they didn't seem to get any easier for either of us. I had discussed my disappointment about never being able to give Shirree away on her wedding day or having grandchildren by her and Brad told me how he had been looking forward to being an uncle one day. Brad loved kids just as Shirree did and he interacted very well with them. We missed Shirree equally. An unknown assailant had shattered our dreams and time had not yet begun to heal.

Detectives working on the case were becoming increasingly frustrated by the apparent reluctance of people to come forward. Appeals guaranteed anonymity. It was reported that a man had called the police emergency number a few days after the murder. It was believed the same man called an Adelaide television newsroom with information relating to Shirree's murder and detectives asked him to call again. They guaranteed to keep his information confidential, but he didn't call back. It was frustrating for both the police and for me when hopes were raised about promising information. During these early days of the investigation a lot of information was coming in but didn't seem to point the police toward Shirree's killer. They had not received much at all to indicate who the killer was.

Under the headline, 'Shirree: A loving life that ended in tragedy',[4] the newspaper described Shirree as a bubbly, blonde schoolgirl, growing into a smiling young woman. A police spokesman said that community safety was at risk with a murderer on the loose and the sooner he was taken off the streets the better it would be for everyone. Police described the murder as 'horrendous', stating that Shirree was set upon viciously and cruelly. 'He [the killer] stripped her of her dignity and it's quite obvious by the injuries that she did everything she could to maintain that dignity—she put up a brave fight.'

'Major crime squads fully stretched—Public afraid to help police solve murders'.[5] These headlines referred to a general item that I found very disturbing. The article reported that police were under severe pressure to catch criminals and prevent more killings after four murders in the space of six weeks. There had been another knifing murder since Shirree's murder, which was the fifth out of the six most recently committed and still unsolved. Police were very concerned that brutal murders were becoming a part of everyday life. Even more disturbing was the comment that police felt the perpetrators of vicious murders were getting better at covering their tracks and leaving few, if any, clues behind.

What is wrong with the mindset of the public? I thought as I threw the paper down in disgust. Were the public becoming so blasé about crimes? I could not help but think that by not coming forward, those who had information that might solve a crime were condoning the actions of criminals.

I was becoming extremely angry. I could not understand how anyone could sit on information that could potentially solve a vicious crime. Was fear a factor? Did people really think when they covered up a crime it would never be discovered? Were they prepared to take that risk? The police can arrange for information to remain confidential, even offering a guarantee of confidentiality, with other avenues of protection available. I wondered what I would do. Would I be fearful of disclosing what I knew about a crime?

Chapter 4

A Kind of Healing

We endured the first Christmas and New Year without Shirree. It brought me down to earth with a thud and my depression returned, bringing a renewal of intense grief. Shirree's birthday in July, only six weeks after her death, was bad enough. Now the family would face Christmas and New Year with a profound sadness. Shirree's sense of fun and celebration would be missing. Surely the New Year would bring better news?

The investigation had come to a standstill. There had been no new information for some time. The police were no closer to an arrest than they had been months ago. Detectives reviewing the material were becoming increasingly frustrated. The identity of Shirree's killer or anything about him was still a mystery. Hopes were built up occasionally but a breakthrough eluded them.

During the lull in the investigation the police spoke to me about the kind of individual who perpetrates a violent crime. What I was told sickened me. Their theories were based on studies of criminal behaviour and long experience. These reports assisted police to profile the characteristics of perpetrators of certain crimes. It sometimes helped in the investigative stage to have an idea of who or what 'type' of person they were looking for.

'Criminal profiling is used in most of the difficult crimes,' I was told. 'It's a relatively new tool that we've only been using for a few years. Expert psychologists and psychiatrists in the field of crime-solving are given details of existing evidence and reports of the type of injuries sustained by a victim. They often come up with an accurate assessment of the type and character of the person who committed the crime.'

Psychological profiling was taking investigators deeper into the mind of the criminal. Understanding the person they were dealing with sometimes helped them to seek clues that might otherwise be overlooked.

'Offender profiling is used in cases where there is no obvious link between offender and victim. Psychologists and police experts study the less visible clues from all available evidence. Experts in profiling use their years of expertise to form an often quite accurate picture of an offender. Some offenders are more likely to be loners than others. Some crims like to brag about their crimes or their expertise in certain areas of criminal activity. Some are plain exhibitionists,' an officer explained.

The fact that Shirree's killer was now thought to be a stranger to her was possibly one of the reasons why the police were having so much difficulty in solving the crime. If the victim is known to the killer it is more likely to be a crime of passion created by jealousy or unrequited love. This type of killer usually panics, leaving some clue behind, is more likely to have a conscience and cannot live with what they have done. They will either surrender to police or be relieved when finally arrested and are usually more than ready to confess.

In early 1994 Shirree's best friend, Cjuzide (pronounced Jassida) was interviewed by a journalist. I opened the paper and read the headline, 'Sad plea for a murdered friend'.[6] The news item refreshed people's memories. It was reported that two separate groups of witnesses had seen a group of four or five men with a woman who might have been Shirree during the hours before her disappearance. The article said 'two of the men were supporting her and helping her to stand'.

'We believe not all of the group would have been involved in the murder and we would like those not involved to come forward,' Detective Johnson said. 'Shirree was like thousands of others that go into town on a Friday or Saturday nights and have a few drinks and lots of fun ... unfortunately for Shirree she got into a situation she couldn't handle.' Detective Johnson said the Turner file had not been closed and that police would not forget the murder until the offenders were brought to justice.

Jas (Shirree's pet name for her friend) said it had been difficult to come forward and ask people to remember Shirree but she felt compelled to do so. She didn't want Shirree's murder to be forgotten and issued a plea in the form of a challenge. She appealed to the compassionate side of the person or persons who had information that could solve her best friend's murder. 'I will never understand how this happened, can you?' she asked.

I had become more and more disillusioned as each month passed and Detective Johnson was about to release the rest of the team to work on other cases. Police resources were still stretched to the limit and much of the information received held nothing more than nuisance value. Many of the calls received proved to be hoax calls but still had to be checked thoroughly. It was eventually decided that resources could be better employed elsewhere. I couldn't help feeling empathy with the police. In a last effort to appeal for help Detective Johnson contacted me.

'I want to run something past you, Ken. Have you ever heard of the television program *Australia's Most Wanted*?'

'Yes I have, but I don't know much about it.'

'What they do is re-enact crimes presented to them using information that police give them. The idea is to refresh the public's memory about the specifics. It's a national program and even though Shirree's murder may not be as up-front in the minds of viewers interstate, you just never know. Something could come out of the extra publicity. Frankly, we could use all the publicity we can get.'

'It sounds good. Do you need my okay or something because if that's all you need then go for it.'

'Well, it's not quite that simple. Sure, we want you to be happy about it being presented on air, but they would probably want to interview you and possibly Brad on camera. I wasn't sure you would be open to any more camera interviews. I know you've both been doing it tough.'

'Mick, please don't hesitate to do whatever it takes. It doesn't matter about my doing it tough. I'm fairly certain Brad would agree. We want this bastard caught as much as you do, even more so. From what I can understand about this type of killer he could do it again. I want him off the streets and as far as the media are concerned, I'll survive.'

'That's what I wanted to hear. I'll contact the program's producer. Thanks Ken. I'll let you know when it's all set up. In my opinion it's worth a shot. They've had a lot of success in flushing out offenders in the past.'

I agreed. Anything that would generate publicity and keep the case up front in the minds of the public was worth an attempt. I dreaded the intrusion of the cameras into my life again but my first priority was to see Shirree's killer captured. Whatever it took would be worth it.

The program's producers set up the interview. The re-enactment, using actors closely resembling Shirree and her girlfriends, was filmed in Hindley Street. Footage from previous news bulletins was incorporated into the program. After editing the segment was going to be aired around the country on Thursday 24 March at 8.30 pm. It was prime time television.

I was genuinely impressed by the way the story was presented and I wondered if Shirree's killer would be watching. Promotional advertisements of the segment played for two days before. If Shirree's killer watched television at all it would be hard to miss the fact that his crime was about to be resurrected in the minds of the public. I hoped that those who might be withholding information would be curious enough to watch the program and be moved to finally come forward. If Shirree's killer or any accomplices were feeling comfortable, I hoped their level of comfort would be lessened with the reminder that police were still on the case. The trail was not as cold as they might hope it to be.

After the segment on *Australia's Most Wanted* the police received a few calls but nothing fruitful eventuated. Again our hopes were dashed. Detective Johnson vowed he would not give up until the case was solved.

The seed of an idea had begun to germinate in my mind. For a while I had been entertaining the idea of moving to another state. The memories and constant reminders of Shirree were too much to handle. My marriage to Merrilyn was over and the events of the past months had taken a huge toll on my health. Merrilyn was still refusing to take my calls and letters were returned unopened.

I began to make tentative plans. I knew it would be difficult to leave family and friends but I felt that I could no longer stay in Adelaide. I hoped to convince Brad to go with me. Either way, I was certain I was destined to move to Queensland. I had travelled to Queensland on a business trip returning just a few days before Shirree's murder. I became very ill on my return but I had fond memories of the places I visited while I was there. I had wanted to take Merrilyn and the children on a holiday to the Sunshine Coast in the hope that we could get our marriage back on track, but Shirree's murder and my subsequent ongoing grief put paid to that idea.

I was inexplicably drawn to the area around Noosa Heads. I felt that if I could get away from Adelaide even for a short time I might be less restless and more settled if I was not so emotionally attached. Leaving my family could prove to be the wrong move but I needed to get on with my own life. I couldn't get away from the intense memories. Something always seemed to remind me of Shirree. I couldn't even relax when I was driving around because I would pass a school where Shirree had attended, a workplace where she had been employed, or her doctor, dentist or hairdresser. Dr Williams had warned me that a complete physical and emotional breakdown was not out of the question. I had to stop pushing myself and I had to stop trying to shield my family and let them grieve in their own way.

I had been diagnosed with post-traumatic stress disorder not long after Shirree's death and it manifested in odd ways, aggravating the already established Chronic Fatigue I suffered. 'Remember, Ken, your body is only designed to take so much. The overload that has been forced upon you will catch up with you eventually if you don't take better care of yourself.'

I was a doctor's nightmare. My distaste for taking medication gave my doctors quite a dilemma and my stubborn refusal to take anything that produced side effects severely limited their ability to help me. I hated feeling out of control. The medication might have lowered the effect of emotional stress and physical pain for a short time but as soon as the effect of the medication wore off it returned. A complete change of scene was the only way I could hope for my health to improve.

It had been almost a year since Shirree's funeral and I was still not working. Grief tended to exacerbate my other physical and emotional problems. Merrilyn wasn't interested in returning to the marriage and my instincts told me that if I didn't move soon my health would never improve.

Brad decided to stay in Adelaide. He had a steady job; he was playing football and didn't want to let his team mates down. I realised that it would not be in Brad's best interest to uproot himself from the only real security he had left. He needed the stability of friends and extended family.

As the days passed my plans began to firm. I became more certain that this was the right move. Brad's twenty-first birthday was approaching in early May and I decided to celebrate with him before leaving.

The only problem I had besides leaving Brad was leaving Shirree. I had visited her grave every now and then since the funeral but now I was leaving her for quite a long time. She would always be in my heart but it was hard to get used to the idea that when I needed to spend a few quiet moments at the grave I would not be able to.

The media discovered I was leaving. A journalist from *The Advertiser* went with me to Shirree's grave. It was a poignant interview, handled with compassion. Surrounded by the beautifully appointed rose gardens at the cemetery I spoke with the journalist about my reasons for leaving Adelaide. 'It's not running away from our responsibilities but facing them in a different place … It's been very difficult. People are frightened to talk about what happened because they are worried about how we will react. Everywhere we go, people recognise us and you can tell they feel uncomfortable.'

I placed a bouquet of Shirree's favourite flowers on the grave. It was sad that people were afraid of what my reaction would be. All I really wanted was normal interaction with people. It was much better for me to discuss the situation openly than to dance around the subject.

I looked tenderly at the photograph of Shirree inlaid on her headstone. 'I guess I have tended to withdraw from any social interaction. I can't handle social situations yet. Shirree's death has deeply impacted so many people.'

'I know that Shirree's mother has not been well, Ken. Do you know how she is coping?' the reporter asked.

'Christine is still having great difficulty in dealing with Shirree's murder. Just as we all are. I guess a parent feels this kind of grief in a different way. I'm continually amazed at just how many people are still suffering. Some of her friends contact me from time to time and even though it's been a long time, they are still hurting deeply. I wonder where it will all end?'

We stood in front of Shirree's grave talking quietly while a photographer discreetly took pictures. 'I don't want anyone to forget about Shirree's murder and the fact that her killer has not been caught yet. He should be constantly reminded that the police will not close the case until he is arrested and brought to justice.'

I had the same feelings about people who must have known something that would help solve the mystery of Shirree's murder. I didn't want them to rest in the belief that their part in this scenario was safely hidden forever. I still hadn't come to terms with the fact that these people, whoever they were, didn't seem to have any moral values at all. 'Why haven't they come forward? They certainly don't seem to care about what they are putting me and my family through.'

After the interview I stood before my daughter's grave. The journalist quietly retreated and left me alone to say goodbye. I looked at the photograph again and realised that Shirree would always be twenty-two years of age, not quite twenty-three. She would forever remain young and beautiful and I vowed never to forget one moment of the time I had been blessed with.

Memories flooded back as I stood immersed in quiet reflection. Surrounded by the peaceful setting of perfectly manicured lawns and superbly kept rose beds I became lost in my memories. As the perfume of the roses drifted around me on the gentle breezes I said goodbye to Shirree. 'I will never forget you, my little girl. I have to leave for a while but you'll always be close to me, here in my heart.'

I felt a profound sense of serenity settle over me as if I had gained Shirree's approval. Suddenly I knew she would want this for me. All my doubts and fears about moving were dispelled in one touching moment. I took a last lingering look at the photograph on the headstone, blew a kiss to my daughter and walked slowly back to the car.

The following morning the article appeared in *The Advertiser*. I read it with a feeling of great sadness, knowing that this chapter of my life was coming to an end. I also realised the sadness would soon be replaced by the excitement of a new start in a new state where the memories were not so hurtful. I was looking forward to new challenges, meeting new friends and beginning a kind of healing.

Detective Johnson promised to keep me informed of developments. 'The case will not be closed until we find the bastard,' he promised. I knew the stalling of the case really annoyed him. 'Don't give up, Ken. I assure you I will not rest until I find him.'

'I will never give up, Mick,' I said. 'I'll keep praying for that elusive piece of information to be found that will crack it open for us. I know I can trust you to do everything you can.' My anger burned. 'I'm still having a huge problem with this. Somebody, besides Shirree's killer, knows something. The contempt I feel for these people scares me.'

There was another aspect that worried me. What happened to the murder weapon? Knives were found and handed in to the police, some from the general area around where Shirree was murdered, but all of them had been eliminated after forensic testing. 'I can't understand why there has been no DNA found. Do you think this bastard cleaned up the area? What could he have done to remove DNA from the scene or from Shirree? I really don't understand any of this.'

'Ken, the Coroner's report stated there was no DNA. There were twigs and leaves found on Shirree's clothing but no fibres. There was no saliva, no semen, no sweat and no blood. Nothing. Maybe he did clean up. He's cut her clothing so it looks like his intention was to rape her. But something else happened. Maybe she woke up to what he was doing and tried to stop him. I don't know. There are any number of scenarios we could look at.' Detective Johnson was just as mystified as I was.

It was time to try to put some of it behind me. I was about to embark on a new journey. I had to leave it with Detective Johnson and the police and trust that very soon the vital piece of evidence would surface.

I found it especially difficult to leave Brad in Adelaide. I avoided prolonged goodbyes when I could but my closest family and friends were not going to let me off the hook that easily. As I drove along the highway I found I enjoyed the solitude, listening to favourite music, enjoying my own company. When I needed rest, I stopped at motels along the way.

Arriving in Noosa Heads I rented a comfortable house. I found a church and met many new friends. I surfed, swam, sunbaked, played a little golf and tennis, beginning to feel human again. The nightmares subsided, although they never left me completely.

My newfound friends, both in the church and outside, although aware of my grieving over Shirree and the manner of her death, kept me busy socially. Until now I had felt inadequate in a group because people were trying not to upset me and tended to avoid talking about Shirree's death, making social occasions very uncomfortable.

I renewed acquaintance with people I had met on the business trip just before Shirree's murder and was able to fill the days with positive experiences. I was well accepted and although the subject of Shirree's murder was brought up on occasions it seemed a little easier to talk about it as time passed. My new friends were just as concerned about the status of the investigation as old friends back in Adelaide and I was very grateful for their interest and support. I began to notice small changes for the better in my health—my panic attacks subsided some-what and I had fewer sleepless nights. Life took on new meaning. I met a group of kids from the church who were instrumental in a rapid pro-gression of my healing. The youth group leader and his wife became firm friends and suggested I help with the group. It wasn't a difficult decision. They seemed to like me and I interacted well with the kids. I was soon accepted as a leader without any problem.

We walked the parks and beaches around Noosa Heads, played games and went swimming in the pool at my new house. The youth leaders regularly scheduled outings to other towns around the Sunshine Coast. We were constantly on the lookout for new, interesting and healthy activities to experience. The group kept my mind from dwelling on my troubles and I found a new lease on life. I had not forgotten Shirree or anything about her murder. It just felt less intense.

Ten-year-old Danielle became very special to me. She was a bubbly, blonde, blue-eyed bundle of energy who reminded me of Shirree. I 'adopted' Danielle with her mother's full approval. I learned a lot from the kids about living life to the fullest and began to feel like I wanted to plan for the future. I didn't want to just play around in the sun and surf forever, as appealing as the idea was. I wanted to look into the possibility of speaking to small groups, especially high school kids, about my experiences. My idea was to create an awareness of the dangers of living a fast lifestyle and I hoped to instil some commonsense ideals in young people to help them in situations they were not equipped to handle or had no experience in dealing with.

Day by day, I became more entrenched in the easygoing lifestyle of the area. I felt more and more accepted and although still deep in grief I was beginning to think that there could be an acceptable future ahead of me. Maybe I *could* function as a real person and not just as the father of a murdered daughter. I understood that it might be difficult for some people to relate to the situation and discovered that it was nearly impossible for people to know exactly how I felt. Unless they were able to walk a mile in my shoes they would never fully understand where I was at any given time.

Chapter 5

A Break in the Case

It was another beautiful day. The sun was shining brightly and a warm breeze wafted through the house as I checked the mail and tried to decide whether to stay at home and catch up on some work or go play a round of golf. The pool needed vacuuming and there were other odd jobs that needed to be done.

I was just about to start the work when the mobile phone rang. I heard long-distance beeps. 'Hello, Ken Turner speaking,' I said, a little tentatively.

I heard a familiar voice on the other end of the line. 'Ken, it's Mick Johnson, Adelaide CIB.'

My heart skipped a couple of beats. 'Yeah, Mick, how are you doing?'

'I have some good news, I think. There's been a breakthrough in the case and I've got the men back on the investigation full time.' I held my breath in anticipation. 'A fresh lead came to our attention recently, although I can't tell you much at this point. But, if all goes as well as I expect it to, we will be making an arrest for Shirree's murder in the next two weeks.'

I was still holding my breath. I was stunned. I found it hard to take in the news; so much time had elapsed since Shirree's murder. 'That's fantastic news. I have so many questions. What the hell happens now? Do you know the guy? How did you find him?' My head was spinning. I was ecstatic but reluctant to hear who the offender might be. I knew I wouldn't cope very well if it were somebody I knew.

'I can't tell you who he is yet, but to put your mind at ease it is most unlikely Shirree would have known him so I doubt you would either.'

'Thank God, Mick. That's one of the things that really bothered me. I know you guys were of the opinion in the beginning that Shirree might have known him. I don't know how I would react if it was somebody I knew.'

'You're right, we did think she might know him. I'm glad for your sake that it appears she didn't. It almost definitely seems to be a random pick-up. He probably stalked her because she was vulnerable and on her own. I have to ask you to keep this information to yourself for the time being, Ken,' Johnson asked, 'at least until the arrest is made. But in all fairness I wanted you to know first.'

'I understand. Thanks for letting me know, Mick, but I need to know as soon as you make the arrest so I can call my family. I don't want Brad to hear it through some other source and I'd like to be the one to tell my mother ... and Shirree's mother as well. I owe them that much.'

'That's fair enough. I'll keep in touch and let you know as soon as I know anything for certain. I'd estimate at this stage it shouldn't take much more than a couple of weeks.'

I breathed a sigh of relief. Shirree's killer was about to be arrested. I didn't know how I was going to keep the news quiet but I had given my word and Detective Johnson needed strict confidentiality.

The inner pain I'd felt for over two years would soon be replaced by something different. Or would it? I wondered if there would be any real satisfaction to be gained from the killer's arrest. I suspected there was still a very long road ahead but this was the first step and I was so excited I wanted to shout for joy.

The horror of Shirree's death and its impact had never been far below the surface and returned as I realised what an arrest would mean. The trauma my family had already been through would be resurrected once more. Media attention, which had been pushed into the background over the past year or so, would intensify.

My thoughts turned into unanswered questions. What kind of person would murder a vulnerable, innocent girl? How could the killer have lived with what he had done for the past two years? Was it an impulsive act? If so, why didn't the coroner find any DNA evidence either at the murder site or on Shirree's body?

The police felt that it was possible the murder was a 'thrill kill'. I was nauseated by the thought but the evidence at the scene pointed strongly toward something strange. There was a sexual assault of some kind but she had not been raped. Did she realise what her killer was trying to do? Did he panic when she fought with him? The same questions had rolled around inside my head for more than two years. I couldn't help but think about what my daughter went through before her death or the terror she must have felt. What were her last thoughts as the life ebbed slowly from her body? I'd imagined the scene over and over again in the past. I could hear Shirree's cries for help as she fought to hold onto her life. I imagined her clutching her chest trying to stem the flow of blood her damaged heart was pumping out, her terror compounded by the feel of the sticky dampness of the blood soaking through her clothes.

She was a brave young woman. She must have had to draw on every ounce of guts and determination to fend off such a frenzied attack. She would have had to remain still, in life-threatening physical pain, pretending to be dead while her attacker escaped. Did her killer check if there was anything to link him to his crime or did he leave in a panic? Did she realise she was dying? I could only imagine the fear she must have felt in the last moments of her life. The hopelessness when she found nobody home at the house where she staggered for help.

I tried not to dwell on my thoughts but it was increasingly difficult to turn them off with the prospect of having to face a trial. I hoped the killer would have the decency to admit his crime once he was arrested and so lessen the court time needed to end this nightmare. Eventually Johnson phoned. The arrest had been made.

'Has he been jailed?' I asked.

'He's not going anywhere,' Johnson replied. 'He's no stranger to the inside. He has a long record. He's in Pentridge on other related matters.'

'Related matters! What the hell does that mean?'

'Just trust me, Ken. He's not going anywhere. Look, I'll keep you informed but for now that's all I can tell you.'

I was flabbergasted, but I had to put my feelings of outrage aside. I needed to contact Brad and the family before they heard about the arrest through the media. I made several phone calls to close family and several of Shirree's closest friends. I asked them to inform anybody else they could think of. They all had questions but I didn't have the answers.

Finally, Johnson called again, revealing the identity of the man who had been arrested for the murder. His name was Frank Mercuri and the police were in the process of applying to the government to have Mercuri extradited to South Australia from Victoria.

The wheels of justice can grind very slowly. The news in mid-October 1995 that Frank Mercuri had been arrested and extradition proceedings started was most welcome, though in this case it seemed the wheels had ground to a complete standstill. It wasn't as though Mercuri had to be brought in from halfway around the world. It was only an extradition from the next state but it took almost twelve months to have Mercuri transferred from Victoria to South Australia.

I understood that extraditing a prisoner from one state to another could be delicate but I was disgusted and very unhappy it was taking so long. Finally, a fax from the Victorian Department of Justice dated 20 July 1996 arrived at the office of the South Australian Attorney-General. An agreement to the request for transferring Frank Mercuri had been reached. Rumours surfaced that Mercuri was trying to escape custody to avoid facing the South Australian courts and extra security arrangements were made to halt any escape attempt.

I stayed in constant contact with Detective Johnson. I discovered that late in August 1995 a call had come in to the Major Crime Squad office. Detective Senior Constable Bill Cunningham took the call. The caller insisted his identity remain anonymous. Detective Cunningham promised that police would do their best but they would need to speak to him personally. Cunningham's amiable nature convinced the informant to meet face to face.

Detective's Johnson and Cunningham arranged a secret meeting very late on a cold August night 1995. The informant told them he had overheard a conversation about the Shirree Turner murder and gave names of men he said were involved. The information he provided steered police toward a group of friends and associates of a man named Frank.

The information was too good to dismiss but because detectives had received several hoax calls in the past a decision was made to treat the new information with caution. Detective Johnson and his team commenced an investigation into the group who met regularly at the Albert Street pool hall.

For two weeks they tested and checked the information and finally planned a synchronised scoop of several members of the group. On 16 September several teams of detectives visited the homes of those initially targeted. Interviews took place at different police departments over the metropolitan area so that no collaboration could take place. Several statements were taken. Information gathered from the first group meant more of the group needed to be interviewed as soon as they became implicated.

Details about Frank Mercuri's alleged confession to two friends, and other bits of information, fitted into the missing spaces of the puzzle. The police concluded their next step was to interview Mercuri himself. Detectives were further astonished to learn that Mercuri was in jail awaiting sentence for another crime. Mercuri refused to speak to police at first but was eventually arrested. The Adelaide detectives had to work on extradition proceedings to get him transferred.

I called Mick Johnson. 'The frustrating bit for us is the red tape involved,' he told me. 'It might take more time than we anticipated getting Mercuri extradited. If we need you to come back in a hurry, I assume you'll be willing to do that?'

Ten months later, Detective Johnson called. The first of the court hearings was set for 18 August 1997. My return to Adelaide was both happy and sad. I was very happy to be reunited with my family, especially Brad, but the circumstances were sad. I could still see hurt on the faces of family and friends. They were reassured that, at least on the surface, I was not displaying too much damage. Underneath though, it was a different story.

One of my first priorities was to meet with the police to find out in greater detail what led to the arrest of Frank Mercuri. There was a possibility I would have to meet the accused man and the feelings I had about such a meeting were entirely personal. I wanted to be prepared.

I made an appointment to see Mick Johnson. I sat quietly in Johnson's office as he reviewed all that had taken place as he brought me up to speed on the status of the police investigation. Johnson told me exactly what the Albert Street pool hall group had told the police.

I was stunned that Mercuri had spent most of his adult life behind bars. His crimes ranged from petty theft and stealing cars to violence, on occasions causing injury to some of his victims. It was not a pretty story.

We discussed my feelings about the individuals who could have ended the nightmare almost four years ago. The police were of the same opinion. The waste of time and resources and some of the hell that my family had been through could have been avoided had they come forward within a few days of the murder.

'What kind of morals do these people have? How could they dismiss what they knew as of no consequence? How could they allow my family and me to suffer as we have done all this time? Don't we matter?' My questions were all valid and hung in the air like a dark cloud. Johnson shrugged his shoulders. What could he say? It was obvious there was no thought given by them, other than to save their own skin.

I tried to put myself into their shoes but to me being an accessory to a crime was as bad as committing a crime. What was missing in the character of those who kept the information to themselves in the face of my suffering family? What they had done was condone the heinous crime of murder.

I could not understand why Shirree would have gone with Mercuri. She had consumed too much champagne and was probably incapable of realising the danger. It was unusual for Shirree to be so intoxicated. Even so, her killer had taken advantage of a vulnerable girl, virtually abducted her, attempted to rape her and then taken her life. It was so senseless. She was probably incapable of identifying him. So why kill her? Something didn't add up. There was something wrong with this story and I was determined to get to the bottom of it.

Chapter 6
The Committal Hearing

Monday morning 18 August 1997 dawned, a typical late winter's day. It was as grey outside as the mood I was in. It was still cold; clouds hung low in the sky threatening to burst. I should have been excited but instead I was feeling pressure. I'd waited a long time for this day but for a very good reason my mood was sombre. It was the day I might come face to face for the first time with the man accused of murdering Shirree. It was the day the committal hearing was due to commence.

A committal hearing is heard before a stipendiary magistrate who decides whether a prima facie case has been proven and should be heard in a higher court. Witnesses are called to give evidence, sworn to tell the truth, examined and cross-examined by attorneys. The evidence is documented and signed by the witnesses. If the magistrate deems a trial should take place, the depositions are forwarded to the Attorney-General. An indictment formulates the charge and the accused is committed to trial. In the case of murder, the Supreme Court is convened.

No jury is involved in a committal hearing. The accused can elect to have a full hearing in order to have the opportunity of cross-examining prosecution witnesses. It is a good way to determine more about the evidence against an accused than would be possible from statements alone, but ultimately the prosecution only needs to present enough evidence to prove that a higher court trial is required.

As it turned out I was not permitted to hear any of the evidence. I had been asked to stand by as a character witness for Fabio should it become necessary. Although I was happy to testify on Fabio's behalf, I was also frustrated that I would have to wait outside. I desperately wanted to see Mercuri's reaction to the testimony of his friends in Adelaide first-hand.

The Director of Public Prosecution (DPP), Paul Rofe, was not overly confident. Rofe knew he could prove that a criminal court trial was in order but the witnesses were unreliable. Several of them had lied to police. Their stories were weak and a good defence attorney would be able to use their lies against them. Mercuri's Defence Counsel, Lindy Powell, was one of the best. Her reputation preceded her and I tried not to feel negative. I was certain the police had the right man but I had picked up on the vibes from the Prosecutor.

I looked through a small window in the door of the courtroom and saw the man accused of murdering my daughter sitting in the dock. I had mixed emotions about seeing Mercuri in person for the first time. I had seen a few photographs but here was Mercuri in the flesh. I knew that sooner or later I might have to be in the same room as him but I was relieved my first glimpse was at a discreet distance. I was better able to gauge what my reaction might be when, and if, we came face to face.

From what I could tell, the accused looked like any other young man. I don't quite know what I expected but from what I could see he looked too young to be facing murder charges. He sat quite still in the dock, was neatly dressed, and at times looked a little bewildered. I was a little surprised that my reaction wasn't the burning anger or righteous indignation some of my friends thought I should have. My friends and relatives knew that because of my beliefs I could not entertain thoughts of retribution, but they still could not understand why I did not display any anger. They couldn't comprehend how I could forgive the killer of one of my children. They wanted revenge and they wanted someone to pay for killing Shirree. They couldn't see that it would not bring her back and holding onto the anger would end up being be detrimental to their own wellbeing.

Detective Johnson had told me that Frank Mercuri was not a nice character. I knew that he had a long criminal history and had been told about some of his past crimes. I was not trying to downplay the seriousness of Mercuri's crimes but I knew how fundamentally wrong it was to entertain the same thoughts my friends had about what had happened to Shirree. Even after explaining why I had chosen to forgive this man, some of them still openly spoke of revenge. They were angry. I was angry about what had happened to Shirree, but I knew that out of control anger wasn't going to do anybody any good.

At that point in time I still trusted the justice system. I had been told enough about Mercuri, about the police investigation, about what the police thought and about what his friends had said about him to be convinced that the evidence was there to convict him. I tried not to pre-judge Mercuri. The law said that he was innocent until proven guilty and I had to trust that the system would take care of Mercuri. What if he was innocent? How would I feel if Mercuri was proven to be completely innocent? I was convinced I had to run with innocent until proven guilty. I'd had a lot of time to think about where I stood in my beliefs and even with knowledge about the character of the man accused of murdering my daughter I had a naïve belief that the system would work it out and that justice would prevail.

I was able to observe the demeanour of the other witnesses. Most of them seemed as nervous as I was although I suspected not for the same reason. There was a lot of pacing around, checking watches, fidgeting hands and whispered conversations with concerned relatives or friends. Advice seemed to go unheeded as the pacing, checking, fidgeting and whispering continued unabated. The smokers smoked one cigarette after another while they waited.

Preliminary matters were dealt with followed by the reading of the charge. The accused made his first official plea of 'not guilty'. I was well prepared for this. I had been told before the hearing how Frank Mercuri intended to plead. Although I hoped deep down Mercuri would do the honourable thing and change his plea, I was not really surprised when he didn't.

Each witness is required to swear an oath on the Bible. If a witness objects they can make an affirmation. A witness who chooses to make an affirmation rather than swear on a Bible is required to state, 'I do solemnly and sincerely and truly declare and affirm that the evidence I will give shall be the truth, the whole truth, and nothing but the truth'. A witness swearing an oath is required to actually take the Bible into their hands and state, 'I swear to tell the truth, the whole truth, and nothing but the truth, so help me God.'

I wondered if the courts actually took it for granted that the use of the Bible is fully understood by all who take the oath. Telling untruths in court is in fact perjury, and the consequence can be a term of imprisonment. I wondered if most witnesses really thought about what they were swearing and whom they were swearing by. Did people make an oath just because it was expected of them?

Michael Mangos was the first witness called to give evidence. Mangos was an acquaintance of Shirree's and said he had seen her in Hindley Street in the early hours of the morning she was murdered. He saw Shirree talking with a girl he did not know and a man whom he thought resembled her former boyfriend although he only glanced at the group. He was not in the mood to talk and kept walking. The time was 2 am.

The next witness, Scott Schinella, was one of the group targeted for questioning after the police received an anonymous phone call. Schinella gave the police three separate statements. It was clear he did not want to give evidence and his body language showed extreme nervousness. In evidence, Schinella told the court that he and a friend were in Mercuri's apartment in the early hours of Sunday 6 June 1993. Schinella told the court of how Mercuri came in 'hysterical, intoxicated and untidy looking', pacing about the room muttering, cursing and swearing. Schinella alleged that Mercuri told him he had stabbed a girl. Shocked by this confession and having no wish to be involved, Schinella made excuses and left. As he was leaving he heard Mercuri ask to be driven downtown. Schinella said he kept quiet about what he knew because he was afraid. His weak excuses were pathetic. Defence Counsel was unimpressed.

Schinella's testimony was followed by that of Chris John Thallas, another member of the group interviewed at the same time as Schinella. Thallas worked as an apprentice mechanic at a petrol station where Mercuri occasionally worked on a casual basis. Thallas claimed Mercuri came to the petrol station on the morning after the murder 'all stressed out' and told Thallas he had stabbed a girl. Thallas was not happy after hearing the confession but continued to see Mercuri until Mercuri returned to Melbourne in June 1993.

Thallas and his girlfriend, Jacqueline Schilling, were in the city on the night of the murder. They saw Mercuri talking with a woman the night Shirree died. Mercuri had asked Thallas if he could understand what she was saying as she was intoxicated and speaking a language Mercuri said he couldn't understand. Thallas told Mercuri he couldn't help him. He didn't want any hassles with his girlfriend.

Thallas did not see Mercuri again that night and gave a vague description of the woman. Defence Counsel thought it was interesting that neither Thallas nor Schinella had spoken about what Mercuri told them either with each other or with anybody else. Counsel was amazed this event did not even rate a discussion between Thallas and his girlfriend.

With persistent probing, Thallas admitted to 'maybe a word or two' with 'maybe some of his friends' on 'maybe a couple of occasions'. Both witnesses used fear as an excuse to justify their behaviour. Both witnesses were afraid to tell the truth.

Thallas's girlfriend, Jacqueline Schilling, described the woman seen with Mercuri in Rosina Street in more detail, differing with Thallas on several points. She said the woman 'had blonde hair with lighter streaks, was wearing dark coloured clothes and had a pendant around her neck. She was probably about twenty and her hair was longer than shoulder length.' The hairstyle was described as 'boofy' or 'big hair'. The woman was 'a bit intoxicated and slurring some of her words'. The witness didn't notice a handbag but stated that 'she had something at her feet that might have been a handbag'.

Schilling had been unhappy about police insistence that she help with their inquiries. Schilling stated she was 'having a bit of a hissy fit' at the time of the police interview because she had to cancel two engagements, a Greek lesson she didn't want to miss and her mother's birthday party.

'Were you still "a bit hissy" when you gave your statement to the police?' Defence Counsel inquired.

'No, not really. I realised the police were just doing their job.'

Ms Schilling denied Thallas discussed the murder with her prior to the day she made her statement. Court adjourned following Ms Schilling's evidence.

That night I watched the television news. A short item covered the events. I had no appetite and was exhausted so I took a hot shower and retired for the night. I hoped to be able to switch off my thoughts but

I ended up tossing and turning all night. The medication I'd reluctantly taken had no effect.

Early the next morning I picked up the newspaper. I was faced with a picture of Shirree taken on the last night of her life and a photograph of Frank Mercuri in police handcuffs, hanging his head. I looked long and hard at the man accused of murdering my daughter and read the article. It reported how Schinella and Thallas had both told the court that Mercuri had confessed to each of them at separate times.

Something compelled me to read every item published and watch every news report in the hope of finding out why this had happened to Shirree. I wondered if I would ever know the real reason and if I did find out, what then? Would knowledge bring closure to this episode of my life? How would I ever really get over Shirree's death? Could I ever forget that my daughter was murdered?'

I arrived back at court the next day in plenty of time. The witnesses were gathering outside the courtroom. The whole building seemed to be buzzing with activity. My mother and sister were waiting in the foyer and I spoke with them briefly before court was called into session.

Julian Berti, the first witness for the day, told the court he was in Mercuri's apartment with Scott Schinella when Schinella alleged Mercuri confessed to a murder. The Berti family was known to have history with Mercuri and had cause to be grateful to him. Julian's older brother Ricardo Berti was serving time at Ararat in Victoria. In an earlier statement to police, Berti's mother told police that Frank had saved Ricardo's life. The Berti family was naturally very grateful. When Mercuri was due for release Ricardo suggested that he go to Adelaide to avoid the heat of 'police harassment'. Ricardo also asked his younger brother Julian to 'look after Frank' when he arrived.

Julian Berti met Mercuri at Keswick railway station and took him to his parent's home where he stayed for several weeks. Berti then rented an apartment in Chambers Street for Mercuri's benefit. Berti paid the bond and rent to begin with until Mercuri could contribute toward expenses. Julian's mother provided crockery, furniture and other items. Julian Berti, by his own admission, spent a good deal of time in the company of Frank Mercuri at the apartment. They hosted numerous drinking sessions, barbecues, socialising with girls and marijuana parties.

Police interviewed Julian Berti on 10 October 1995. Berti told police that Mercuri came back to the apartment in Chambers Street in a highly agitated state the night of Shirree's murder. Berti admitted he had been drinking heavily and was annoyed by the noise Mercuri was making. He just wanted him to 'shut up'. He denied hearing anything about Mercuri stabbing a girl. Berti thought he had been in a fight and was just 'a bit pissed off'. He said he didn't take much notice of what Mercuri said.

Berti stated that he was too drunk to remember if he drove Mercuri downtown or not and had no memory of tossing three handbags out of the window on the way. The Prosecutor did not place any significance on this witness's story. Police were very skeptical about the truth of his statement and indicated they felt he was not telling 'all he knew'. The Prosecutor declined to examine the witness. It was a waste of the court's time.

Defence Counsel however, wanted Berti's story told and the court heard that members of the group who visited the apartment regularly considered it their meeting place. It was a 'drop in any time' arrangement. Berti did not deny he was in the apartment on the night when Mercuri had come home in an agitated state or that it was a possibility they left together to go downtown. However, he categorically denied hearing anything about Mercuri stabbing a girl.

Steve Raftellis was the next witness. In an earlier statement to police Raftellis had said he knew and associated with the group, including cousins with the same name. The two Thallas men were known amongst the group as Big Chris (who had testified earlier) and Little Chris. Scott Schinella and Julian Berti were also named as friends.

Raftellis told police he had not associated with Mercuri very much because he didn't like him. According to Raftellis, 'Mercuri was a person who took advantage of others and acted too much like a big shot and a tough person'. He recalled seeing Mercuri downtown on one occasion and thought it was around two years prior to his interview.

He said he was with a group of friends when a utility Mercuri was driving pulled up near them. He recognised the utility as one of the vehicles from the petrol station where Big Chris worked. Thallas's cousin (Little Chris) got out of the vehicle and asked to join them. The vehicle, with Mercuri and a woman—whom he described as young, with long hair to the shoulders—drove off toward West Terrace. Raftellis said that was the last time he'd seen Mercuri and he believed Mercuri left Adelaide shortly after.

Three or four weeks prior to making his statement Raftellis and some of his friends were visited by detectives who spoke about the murder of Shirree. Thallas's cousin (Little Chris) told him that 'the cops were talking about the night they had seen each other downtown'. Little Chris was referring to the night he had joined them when Mercuri and the woman drove off alone.

The prosecution declined to examine the witness. Between giving his statement and the committal hearing something had changed Raftellis's mind. When examined by the defence, Raftellis stated he had changed his statement because he 'only saw the back of the heads of the driver and the woman as the utility drove off and couldn't really identify them because he didn't get a good look at them'. He [said he] didn't suspect Mercuri had anything to do with the murder until police questioned the group.

Raftellis also denied having a conversation with Schinella in which it was alleged he told Schinella he 'saw Frank with the girl who got murdered'. The new version of Raftellis's story, given as testimony at the committal hearing, was in direct contradiction to his first statement to police. In his first statement Raftellis made three distinct observations. Firstly he said, 'I know the girl had long hair down to the shoulders.' Secondly, 'I saw that the driver of the ute was Frank' and thirdly, 'Chris [Little Chris] was referring to the night that he got out of the vehicle driven by Frank.'

These statements were definite when given to the police in the first instance. What happened in the interim for such a drastic change of mind to have occurred? Why was he so definite and detailed in his statement to police and then very unsure when giving evidence at the committal hearing? Why would the witness fabricate a story in the first place about recognising Mercuri as the driver of a utility that he knew belonged to the petrol station where his friend Thallas worked? Why would he describe the woman as having long hair down to the shoulders in the first instance if he didn't actually see her?

Raftellis's version of events needed Little Chris's verification and Little Chris refused to tell the police anything, stating he knew nothing about the murder. Little Chris disappeared soon after his interview and could not be subpoenaed to testify during any of the hearings.

The police felt that some of the so-called fabricated stories were a little too elaborate to have been simply made up. They believed there was an element of truth to all of the stories but none of the group could tell the whole truth. They were playing a dangerous game whatever the truth was.

They had not given a second thought to my family. Nor did they have any conscience about what had happened to Shirree. To have told a story even vaguely implicating Mercuri, then reneging, suggested there was something terribly amiss about their stories. Did the members of this group know more than they were willing to tell? The police thought so. I thought so. The prosecution thought so. So why were they not coming clean with what they knew?

Fabio Bertagno, Shirree's ex-boyfriend, signed a statement in October 1995. It was a reduced version of his interviews with police in June 1993. The police were impressed by the fact that Fabio was more than willing to answer questions and cooperate fully from the outset. He was one of the early suspects.

'Shirree and I were involved in a relationship for about five years. She ended it in October 1992,' Fabio said. Although he was unhappy about the relationship ending, the court heard how he and Shirree had re-established a friendship after he realised it was his attitude causing the problems between them. They remained friends until her death.

'Shirree was supposed to meet me at ICA [an indoor sports stadium] that night but she didn't come. I called her home. Her brother told me she was downtown with friends.' Fabio stayed at the stadium until midnight.

When Defence Counsel questioned Fabio she focused on the more volatile side of Fabio's relationship with Shirree. He admitted he disapproved of her going to nightclubs. He and Shirree had several heated arguments. Even after they broke up he let her know he still disapproved of her visiting the clubs and freely admitted that when he didn't have a girlfriend he drank excessively.

The court heard that in November 1992, a month after they broke up, Fabio threatened Shirree with a knife. In her diary Shirree described Fabio as being very drunk at the time. An extract of a diary entry was read out to the court. Fabio responded, 'I can't remember exactly what happened that time but whatever Shirree wrote in her diaries would be correct.'

Defence Counsel, possibly disappointed at Fabio's candid admissions, zeroed in on his disappointment that Shirree had formed a friendship with another man. Fabio was questioned about a confrontation with Shirree while she was parked close to her home with her new boyfriend, Evan. Fabio ordered Shirree to get out of the car several times and Shirree refused. Evan tried to defuse the situation by starting the car and driving away but Fabio punched the front passenger side window with his fist, smashing the glass.

Defence Counsel hammered the point that Fabio's violent episodes were because he was still in love with Shirree and unhappy about the new relationship. Fabio responded, 'After a while I accepted the situation. If Shirree is happy, I am happy.' Although disappointed that Shirree had decided not to go to the netball stadium on the night she was murdered, he waited until midnight, arriving home at 12.30 am.

With Fabio's testimony over I was relieved that I would not be called to testify although I would have truthfully told the court my impression of the man whom Shirree once hoped to marry. Although I could not condone his erratic behaviour and hot-headed attitude I had no doubt that Fabio loved Shirree. I'd wondered fleetingly, in the beginning, whether Fabio might have lost control and done something stupid in anger, but I knew Fabio well enough to trust that he would never have harmed Shirree physically.

Detective Michael Johnson was the final witness. Administrating the investigation, Johnson had headed the task force during both the 1993 and 1995 investigations. As Administration Sergeant he was responsible for the entire investigation once the murder was declared a major crime.

Detective Johnson explained the reason for the non-appearance of Chris George Thallas (Little Chris) in detail. Police involved in attempting to serve him with a subpoena found he had simply disappeared. Inquiries were made in various known haunts but police were of the opinion that Little Chris was deliberately avoiding them. There was an outstanding warrant for his arrest on another matter, possibly an additional reason for absconding.

Detective Johnson told the court that police had interviewed Little Chris early in the second investigation. He avoided answering questions to do with the murder, only admitting that he knew Mercuri and where Mercuri lived. He refused to say any more before consulting with a solicitor. Police received a signed letter through his solicitor stating that Little Chris didn't know anything and didn't wish to be interviewed further on the subject. Evan Grigoris, Shirree's boyfriend, was holidaying in Greece and would not testify.

Detective Johnson gave the court an overview of the investigation. He explained that police had received information about the group of men associated with Frank Mercuri through a person who was subsequently given informant status. The informant had given quite specific details about those alleged to have known of the murder.

Defence Counsel requested a copy of the information given by the informant. She made her intentions clear. She was unimpressed by the manner in which police had conducted parts of the investigation. Defence Counsel claimed that police had 'looked into' and dismissed many of the calls made by individuals claiming to know something about he murder.

Johnson also said that Jacqui Schilling was the only person from the group to actually identify Shirree as the woman she'd seen with Mercuri, albeit from a photograph. Other witnesses had come forward as a result of publicity. Each witness was offered immunity from prosecution in an effort to persuade them to tell the truth.

Court adjourned to allow the magistrate time to review the evidence. I was warned not to put too much hope in the fact that Defence Counsel had not tried very hard to discredit the prosecution witnesses. It was not important to pursue witnesses vigorously at this stage of the proceedings. Both the defence and prosecution knew there was enough evidence for the magistrate to recommend Mercuri be committed to stand trial so they didn't need to play all of their cards. The prosecution, in particular, didn't want every strategy revealed, weak as they were.

'You'll see Lindy Powell's true colours come out before the jury,' I was warned. Defence Counsel's reputation for aggressively defending her clients was well known in legal circles. She was one of the best defence QCs in the State.

As expected, Frank Mercuri was committed to stand trial in the Supreme Court. A trial date was set down for early March 1998, over six months away. It was to be another long wait.

Chapter 7
Waiting

During the time between the committal hearing and the criminal trial I tried to keep busy. I'd long ago ceased trying to harness my thoughts. The more I tried the harder it became and the pressure I was under began to make me more and more depressed. My nightmares returned with a vengeance. I visited my doctor regularly but I'd been required to return to Adelaide where the horror had occurred. Bad dreams and panic attacks were turning my life into a living hell.

Family and close friends were solid in their support. I didn't know how I would have stood the test without their willingness to be there for me as we endured another Christmas and New Year without Shirree. Christmas seemed worse than I remembered from past celebrations. As much as I tried to stand firm, the closer the trial date came the harder it became to hold my emotions in check.

I was in constant contact with DPP Paul Rofe and Detective Johnson. Concerned that the case was very weak, they'd had nothing but grief from the witnesses. Keeping the case on an even keel was becoming more impossible by the minute.

I did a lot of walking along the beach during this time. I found that this helped to clear my head. I was having trouble building new relationships with people and was finding trusting people difficult. I'd had bad experiences in the past with particularly hurtful comments made about Shirree. She was no longer able to defend herself and I felt I had to set the record straight when uninformed comments were made. It was a constant battle not to sink into victim mentality thinking. Having to deal with extra issues demanded energy that I could ill afford to expend.

I visited the Supreme Court building to familiarise myself with the environment around the courts so I would not be overawed by events when the trial began. I'd never had occasion to visit the courts before and I wandered through the halls of justice for an hour, taking in every aspect of the imposing building and the atmosphere inside. By the time the trial was due to start I hoped I would be ready to face the next hurdle.

I hardly slept for several days leading up to the trial. I was discouraged in the lead-up and Paul Rofe was inadvertently the cause. Paul had little choice but to try the case, knowing the difficulties he would face presenting available and admissible evidence. Although determined to put his best foot forward he was up against one of the best defence attorneys in the State and she would be equally determined to gain a 'not guilty' verdict for her client.

'The case is very weak,' Paul told me by phone a few days before the trial was due to begin. 'We are up against it, I'm afraid. The reliability of the testimony of at least half of the witnesses is a definite worry for us. They can't keep their stories straight and I'm certain they haven't told us all they know. We'll do our best with what we've got but it's not going to be a walk in the park by any means.'

Nearly five years had elapsed since the murder and unless some new and dramatic evidence came into their possession or a reversal of attitude from primary witnesses occurred the prosecution faced a very difficult task.

Their entire case relied upon the testimony of witnesses who, for whatever reasons, could not keep their stories straight. If the jury doubted their testimonies, then they could hardly be expected to convict the accused of murder.

The passage of time between the murder and the trial gave a distinct advantage to the defence. The memory of the witnesses would not be as sharp, and recalling specific details might be a problem for them. Schinella, Thallas, Raftellis, Berti and others continued to vacillate about details, which decreased the value of their testimony markedly. I felt sorry for Paul and the prosecution team. They were beginning a trial that would have been an open and shut case had certain individuals come forward with information earlier.

The day arrived for preliminary discussions. Justice EP Mullighan was appointed trial judge and heard Defence Counsel, Lindy Powell, open on the first morning with two applications. It was predictable that she would try to discredit Schinella's testimony. Powell claimed it was difficult to assess which statement was the truth because Schinella changed his mind between the first and second statemements he gave to police. It was also inconsistent with his testimony, which she believed was incredible, and that he changed his story for no satisfactory reason. Which was all true.

Defence Counsel went on to claim that the change of story might have been believable if Mercuri had threatened Schinella or even his girlfriend. But Schinella had not mentioned anything about threats, veiled or otherwise. He was the one 'too scared' to tell the truth. Schinella's inconsistencies produced another problem. The Prosecutor, Paul Rofe, had decided not to call two of the witnesses, Julian Berti and Steve Raftellis. Defence Counsel argued that the reason for this was simply because they did not back up Schinella's story.

The prosecution tried to counter-argue. Why would they call witnesses who changed their stories so dramatically when this would directly refute the testimony of a primary witness, to whom Mercuri was alleged to have confessed? Rofe admitted an opinion had been formed regarding Julian Berti as 'clearly unreliable, if not plainly untruthful'. Various reasons were given including the connection of the Berti family with the accused and the circumstances surrounding the accused coming to South Australia.

Steve Raftellis's credibility was also questioned. In his first statement Raftellis identified Mercuri with a girl in a vehicle in Hindley Street on the Saturday night of Shirree's death. A quite detailed record of the events he saw were given to the police. Then, while testifying at the committal hearing, Raftellis made a complete about-face and flatly denied that an oral exchange about the murder had ever taken place between him and Schinella. Raftellis had changed his story to such an extent that to call him as a witness would have been folly on the part of the prosecutor.

While the magistrate at the committal hearing had decided there was enough evidence for the accused to stand trial, the Prosecutor's problem now was whether the testimony of the witnesses and their alleged knowledge of the crime was admissible.

The second application that Defence Counsel felt should not be raised at trial was the testimony of Jacqueline Schilling and her photo identification of the deceased. Counsel argued that the photo identification procedure had not been conducted correctly and used grounds of unreliability and unfairness.

A request for a preliminary hearing was finally granted. The hearing would determine admissibility of the evidence in question. The judge heard that during the interview with Schilling, Detective Brian Swan and his partner were given details about an encounter with Frank late one night. Schilling told detectives that she and her boyfriend met Frank in a lane downtown. He was with a girl whom Schilling described in detail. She stated that she didn't know Frank's surname but she thought it was similar to 'Mercury', referring to the surname of the rock singer, Freddie Mercury, from the band Queen.

Detective Swan requested a batch of photographs from the Major Crime Office be delivered to Darlington. He selected three photographs of Shirree and placed them on the desk before Schilling. She pointed to one of the photos, stating that the girl looked remarkably like the girl she had seen with Mercuri. She didn't identify Shirree from the photograph primarily used by police for publicity purposes but pointed to another photo of Shirree taken two months prior to her death.

Although the photo identification was conducted in an appropriate manner, Defence felt that Schilling might have been unduly influenced by publicity during the police investigation. Shirree's photograph had been used in almost all of the publicity and her face was particularly well known. She believed the time lapse between the murder and when Schilling was asked to look at photographs would have influenced her decision.

After much debate and discussion over the law as it applied to the case, the Prosecutor agreed the photo identification could not be used as evidence and the Judge concurred. It was another blow to the prosecutor's case. The one positive ID of Shirree couldn't be used in court. Justice Mullighan decided the applications were premature but left the way open for both legal teams to raise the issues again during the trial. Court was adjourned until Wednesday 4 March 1998 at 10 am.

Chapter 8
The Crown vs Mercuri

The wheels of justice seemed to grind along slowly in this case. I could hardly believe it had been nearly five years since the murder. Waiting for Shirree's killer to be arrested was difficult enough but the red tape involved in having him extradited from Victoria, enduring a committal hearing and finally setting a trial date had really taken its toll on my health. I'd wondered more than once if those involved in the justice system ever really considered the feelings and emotions of victims of crime.

I was relieved the trial was soon to commence but the nervous stress I experienced brought back the misery of why we were in court. For several weeks leading up to the trial I relived the horror of Shirree's death and the torment our family had experienced. My vivid nightmares returned. To make matters worse, there was still a possibility I would need to testify as a character witness for Fabio.

I wasn't happy about the possibility of having to be a witness. It meant that I couldn't watch the trial unfold and would have to rely on friends and relatives to be my eyes and ears inside the courtroom. I hoped that I was not asking too much of them. They were carrying their own emotional burdens.

The trial was allocated to Court 6, which could be reached either by elevator or by a magnificent marble staircase rising from the centre of the ground floor to the second level. A huge and quite spectacular stained glass dome high above the centre of the marble staircase was part of the original structure and enhanced the splendour of the building.

During the trial I would be left outside to pace the floor, or wander about looking at the structure of the magnificent building. I remembered it had once been a large department store. Renamed the Sir Samuel Way Building, it now contained the corridors of the justice system. Members of the press gathered each day to report on the day's proceedings. The public gallery was often filled to capacity because the trial held great interest for a lot of people.

Mercuri was ushered into court each day by a sheriff's officer. He sat in the dock dressed in a dark grey suit, tie and creamy yellow shirt. His appearance was typically European with black hair very closely cropped. He looked physically fit and his most distinctive feature were his dark brooding eyes.

At the commencement of each sitting the Clerk of the Court called 'Please stand' as Justice Mullighan walked in to take his place on the bench. Resplendent in his red robe and white wig he entered the court taking his seat facing the legal teams and the public gallery. 'The Crown versus Mercuri' was announced each morning.

Rofe and his assistant were grim-faced while waiting for the proceedings to begin. I was only able to look through a small window in the door of the courtroom to gauge the mood inside. Even though the month of March in Adelaide is traditionally warm I felt the atmosphere inside the court was even colder in contrast. I shivered as I watched the defence team preparing to go into battle for the accused. They looked confident, efficient and ready to go. I could only hope that the prosecution team was ready for the fight that was before them.

As proceedings began the charge was read and the defendant's plea of 'not guilty' entered, followed by Justice Mullighan's first address to the jury pool from which twelve jurors would be selected. Justice Mullighan first estimated the length of the trial to be three or four weeks. 'My role will be to ensure the trial proceeds in accordance with the best principles of fairness.'

Both Defence and Prosecution were given the opportunity to challenge potential jurors and the panel was reduced to twelve people. The final twelve consisted of nine women and three men. The trial was ready to begin.

The Prosecutor opened for the Crown. Paul Rofe outlined the case, step by step. He began the story from the time when Shirree's body was found. 'It is the contention of the Prosecution that Ms Turner's killer is the accused in this cause. We also contend there was no known prior association between Ms Turner and Mr Mercuri.'

Rofe told the court that Mercuri was in the city that night. 'How he met with Ms Turner, got her to the park and what precisely happened there are details known only to the accused.'

The Prosecutor alleged that Mercuri confessed to two of his associates soon after the murder. He went on to say:

An accused always comes into court with a presumption of innocence in our justice system. It is the Prosecution that has the burden of proving the charge of murder. The Prosecution must prove each element of the crime of murder beyond reasonable doubt.

Murder is the deliberate killing of another person, without lawful excuse and with the express intention to kill or cause grievous bodily harm. The Prosecution will rely almost entirely on confessions by associates of the accused, Scott Schinella and Chris John Thallas.

The victim was murdered only one kilometre from the apartment where Mr Mercuri resided. The handbags belonging to the victim and her two friends were found dumped on Marion Road, within a kilometre of the apartment on the downtown side.

The accused was given a knife for his birthday, which was only a few days before the murder. This particular knife was capable of inflicting the wounds found on Ms Turner's body.

The Prosecutor reminded the jury that witnesses would be asked to recall details from nearly five years ago. Because of the time lapse between the murder and the trial he wanted the court to realise that it was not humanly possible to remember exact details over a long space of time.

The crime scene, the post-mortem examination, and the tracing of the movements of the deceased were detailed. It was the duty of the Prosecution to look at things like appearance of the deceased, levels of intoxication, times and general background. The main points from the regenerated police investigation, the alleged confessions by the accused to Schinella and Thallas, and the fact that the murder weapon was never found, were presented as facts of the case. A knife believed to be the same as the one given to Mercuri for his birthday was also submitted. The Prosecutor noted that the knife was of the type that could have inflicted the wounds. The Prosecutor explained the duties of the jurors as it related to the case. He implored the jury to listen to all of the evidence and weigh it up carefully. It was a difficult case and he didn't want the jurors to make up their minds before hearing every piece of evidence he had to present. 'The reality is that we have a brutal, senseless killing of a young girl who was in no condition to defend herself. In law, and in this courtroom, you cannot allow sympathy for Shirree Turner or her family to deflect you from your task.'

Since material the jury would be required to view could be distressing, Justice Mullighan said, 'I want you to be prepared so that when you are given photographs of the deceased, you will be able to view them dispassionately.'

Photographs were taken from every angle where the attack occurred, the house where the victim's body was found and the surrounding area. Even the trail of blood leading from the reserve was detailed photographically. Photographs of the position of the body on the porch and its bloodied condition were shown to the jury and they were required to view a selection of graphic images taken both before and after the autopsy began, with the location of each stab wound marked for identification. Was it possible to view such material dispassionately?

A police helicopter took aerial photographs of the crime scene where the handbags were located and Mercuri's apartment, showing their close proximity. Each piece of evidence was numbered, tendered and admitted as evidence. The testimony of early witnesses contained mostly technical information of police involvement. There was little clarification needed and Defence Counsel declined to cross-examine the early witnesses. A statement from the man who discovered Shirree's body was read to the court. Police had arrived within minutes of his call, assessing immediately that Major Crime should be informed.

There was a request made for an ambulance to be dispatched to the scene and paramedics attached a portable ECG to the body, confirming no sign of life. Communications notified the Major Crime division of Homicide while officers secured the area, sealing the crime scene from curious onlookers. Orange plastic cones placed across Salrak Avenue blocked traffic from entering the street. A police vehicle was placed across the Minchinbury Terrace end to block traffic from entering from that direction. Yellow crime scene tape was erected around the house where the body was found and around the area in the reserve where the victim was attacked. It was established that proper precautions were taken to secure the crime scene and the procedures for gathering evidence were of the highest standard.

The man who found the handbags told the court he had been travelling north along Marion Road near Bus Stop 19 at about 8 am. He noticed a white plastic bag with what appeared to contain more than one lady's handbag scattered on the road in the left lane. He moved into the next lane, executed a double U-turn and parked on the road.

Approaching cautiously he noticed personal papers, driver's licences and sundry make-up items. Placing them into the plastic bag, the kind used to carry groceries from a supermarket, he put them on the floor of the car and continued to his original destination. Later that morning he handed the items in to Darlington Police.

After a break the court heard separately from Sonia and Kirsty about their relationship with Shirree, how they came to be in the city on the night in question and the events leading to the separation. Both stated how it was unusual for Shirree to wander off by herself. Both were told about the murder when they identified their handbags.

Both girls were undeniably devastated by what had happened to their friend, equally mystified as to why Shirree would wander off on her own. The court heard that when Kirsty and Sonia realised Shirree was missing they were initially quite angry. After all, Shirree had taken their handbags with her and left them with no money and no means of continuing their celebration. After looking everywhere they could think of they decided to go home. They took a taxi back to Kirsty's apartment and her boyfriend paid the fare. Sonia stayed the night at Kirsty's because Shirree had her house keys in her handbag. The next morning the girls continued to try and locate Shirree, their annoyance turning to dismay when their handbags were collected from Darlington Police Station

Following Kirsty and Sonia, the women who spoke with Shirree when she left the Charles Sturt Tavern testified. Jasmine and Rebecca were seated outside the Charles Sturt Tavern when a woman approached them from the direction of the Tavern. They were engaged in conversation and noticed she was carrying three handbags.

'She said her name was Shirree and we invited her to join us. Shirree asked me to hold onto a five-dollar note for her, as this was her cab fare home. We suggested she go home and sober up and she agreed. We took her to a taxi stand and Jasmine gave the taxi driver an address and the five-dollar note but Shirree changed her mind. She told us her friend was a taxi driver and he was going to pick her up when she was ready to go home. Shirree asked us to join her but we were hoping to meet friends later so we said goodbye. She headed toward the central downtown area. We didn't see her again.'

Rebecca described Shirree as 'about twenty, looked Australian but her voice sounded Italian by the way she was speaking'. She gave a very accurate description of height, colour and style of hair and clothes. Rebecca and Jasmine couldn't have known that Shirree, because of her long association with Fabio's family, could speak and understand Italian and that the address given to the taxi driver was Shirree's address.

Jasmine woke later that morning to her clock radio and heard that a woman carrying three handbags had been murdered. The three handbags triggered her memory and Jasmine called Rebecca, agreeing to meet at the Hindley Street Police Department. They were then interviewed by detectives who were working on the investigation into Shirree's murder. If only Shirree hadn't changed her mind. She stubbornly refused to go home because the cab driver was not Evan. It was a fatal decision.

The next group of witnesses testified they saw Shirree at various times that morning, followed by Michael Mangos whose evidence echoed what he said at the committal hearing. Mangos testified he saw Shirree with a man resembling her former boyfriend, Fabio, and since he didn't want to talk with Shirree, he ignored her as he passed by.

The Prosecutor arranged for Fabio to be brought into the courtroom. Allowing for differences in hairstyle and clothing, and even though he only glanced at the group, Mangos was certain Fabio wasn't the man he saw talking with Shirree.

Other witnesses said they saw Shirree, but identified her because she was carrying three handbags. Some said she was in the company of an 'ethnic looking guy'. They could have been describing any number of women who may have looked like Shirree, a very pretty girl, with long wavy blonde hair worn fashionably. Shirree was dressed in black, her clothing and jewellery also according to fashion. Nothing stood out about her except that she was carrying three handbags.

My patience was wearing thin. I wanted to hear the witnesses first-hand and couldn't wait for breaks to find out what was going on. It hadn't been necessary for me to testify at the committal hearing and I doubted it would be necessary during this trial. There were others, who knew Fabio better than me, who could have testified, although I realised my testimony on Fabio's behalf would carry a lot more weight. I spent most of the trial talking with the people who were gathered outside of the court.

I wondered how Fabio was feeling as I paced nervously outside. The Prosecutor had indicated that Defence Counsel intended making the most of Fabio's treatment of Shirree to try to shift suspicion away from her client, the reason I was standing by as a witness.

Fabio was very open and helpful. It was obvious the police would suspect he might have had something to do with her death given the volatile nature of their relationship. However, Fabio had nothing to hide. Detectives who interviewed him noted he was always 'cooperative as usual'. He wanted Shirree's killer brought to justice as much as her family did.

'Shirree was not the type of girl to wander off without letting anyone know where she was going,' he'd said to the police. 'She would talk to any male stranger to be polite. She was kind-hearted and trusting to a point, but she wouldn't have gone off with someone she didn't know.' Fabio confirmed what every person who knew Shirree had been saying since her death.

The Prosecutor asked, 'Did you have anything to do with the death of Shirree Turner?'

'No, I didn't,' Fabio replied.

During cross-examination Defence Counsel covered points from Fabio's interviews and statements but with a very different agenda in mind. She tried to use Fabio's bad temper and acts of jealous rage to his disdvantage. Fabio acknowledged these traits, admitting honestly that his heavy drinking contributed to most of the bad behaviour.

Fabio explained that a knife found in his car was a fishing knife. It was returned after forensic testing eliminated it as the murder weapon. Fabio carried a pocket-knife in a pouch on his belt, used in the course of his job inspecting for white ants in and under buildings. It was also eliminated.

Each attack by Counsel was repelled strongly and it was felt that Fabio stood up well under the intense cross-examination that was expressly designed to throw doubt into the minds of the jurors about his alibi. It was the person who gave him the alibi, who was listed to testify next, that gave Defence Counsel the opportunity to lay the foundation for a tiny seed of doubt.

Fabio's mother was called to support his alibi. Lina Bertagno answered the expected questions about Fabio's relationship with Shirree. The court heard Shirree was a regular visitor, sharing many meals with the family. Mrs Bertagno and her husband gave Shirree a twenty-first birth-day party at their home. After the relationship ended they did not speak as often but their special relationship continued.

Fabio's mother had a heavy Italian accent and it was difficult for her to understand some of the questions. The Prosecutor gently guided her through the examination. In halting English she stated she first heard Shirree had died on the Sunday night when I had telephoned Fabio. 'Yes, it was Sunday night. We got tea with my family. The telephone rang. Fabio answered. I asked, "Who is it?" He say, "It's Ken—father of Shirree." '

'When he came out from there I saw him really upset in the face. We ask, "What has happened?" He say, "Shirree is dead. Somebody stabbed her." At the moment I thought he was joking. When I look in the face, you can see it is no joke. Everybody was upset.'

The court heard that Fabio arrived home at 12.30 am on the night of the murder. 'I tell him, "Why you come home late? You said you are going tomorrow at 5 am for motorbike." He don't answer. He go under the blanket. He don't want to listen when I tell him off. I go back to bed.'

Mrs Bertagno said she knew Fabio was home at 3 am because she went to the bathroom. His bedroom was across the corridor and she could see he was asleep. She prepared coffee and sandwiches for him at 5 am and drank a cup of coffee with Fabio and his cousin before they left.

Defence Counsel queried the fact that Fabio told the court he had not spoken to anyone when he came home, but went straight to bed. Fabio's mother, in heavily accented English, had given the court the impression that a conversation had occurred between them. She denied Fabio spoke with her. She said she spoke to him and he ignored her comments, pulling the blanket over his head to indicate he was not listening to her.

Mrs Bertagno didn't sleep well, retiring fifteen or twenty minutes before Fabio arrived home. She got out of bed to go to the bathroom and spoke to him about getting home late, repeating that he ignored her and pulled the blanket over his head indicating he didn't want to listen to her telling him off.

The question irritated the witness. She repeated what was said and explained in no uncertain terms that her 'English might not be so good' and 'after five years her memory about exact words might not be so good', but essentially her testimony was the same.

The Prosecutor objected to repeated questioning about the same incident, indicating that Counsel was harassing the witness. Fabio's mother was not going to change her testimony. Mrs Bertagno backed Fabio's testimony regarding the knives, before Counsel returned to the previous line of questioning. Obviously exasperated, the witness repeated what had transpired between them. 'I told her. He don't answer back. Repeat all the time.'

Fabio, sitting in the courtroom listening to the cross-examination, was fuming. His anger at the insensitivity shown toward his mother was only settled temporarily by the Prosecutor's final question to her.

'Are you telling lies to protect your son?'

'No! I don't protect my son. I know my son is not guilty. If my son is guilty, I don't defend him. To do that to Shirree, that's terrible. I love my son. I never defend my son if he do something like that. I know my son is not guilty,' she said emphatically. Fabio knew that his mother would never lie for him. She would never have tolerated his physically hurting anyone. For as much as she loved him, she also loved Shirree.

Evan Grigoris, the man Shirree was seeing at the time of her death, was next to testify. The court heard how Evan and Shirree did not see much of one another early in the relationship but saw a little more of each other after Shirree and her brother moved into their stepmother's house. However, due to the hours Evan worked it was difficult to see her as often as he might have wanted. They went out occasionally and to his knowledge Shirree did not go out while he was working except when she told him.

Evan saw Shirree early on the afternoon before she died. She said she was going out with friends she had not seen for a while. He suggested she call him on his mobile phone when she was ready and he would take her home. That call never came.

The police checked Evan's job sheet. A petrol station receipt recorded that he purchased fuel in the northern suburb of Blair Athol at 4.26 am.

The petrol station was on the other side of town from the reserve. Evan drove to Hindley Street after finishing work at 5 am to see if he could find Shirree. He assumed she was still partying when he couldn't find her and went home, expecting to hear from her later in the day. Her usual practice was to call him on a Sunday afternoon after he slept.

Evan recalled being woken by his mother sometime during the day and asked whether he'd seen Shirree. When he woke on Sunday afternoon and tried to call Shirree, he got no answer. He kept trying over the next two hours, then phoned her father.

'Shirree was a caring, sensitive woman. She always needed company and was very friendly. She had high morals, was quite intelligent but a bit naïve. She would never go with anyone she didn't know willingly.'

Evan described their relationship as serious but that they were 'taking things very slowly'. He explained that neither of them felt ready for a permanent commitment. The court heard that Evan carried a knife in his taxi for protection. Taxi drivers were vulnerable to robberies and most drivers carried something to use for protection.

The police took his taxi driver's uniform and the knife for forensic examination with photographs of him and Shirree together and the clothing he was wearing in the photographs. His taxi was impounded and examined.

Defence Counsel asked, 'Did you ever converse with any of your passengers about Shirree's murder?'

'Only in general conversation.'

'Were you angry about her going out with her friends that night?'

'No. I wasn't angry about her going out but I was very upset and angry about what happened to her,' he stated.

Counsel suggested some of Evan's passengers had reported to police what he'd said concerning Shirree's murder. 'Well, if they did the police didn't speak to me about it,' Evan replied.

Counsel then accused Evan of having threatened Shirree in the past. A passage from Shirree's diary was read out to Evan when the police interviewed him. Shirree had written in her diary about a night she had spent with Evan and his cousin when they first met. The court heard the extract:

> Then they started having bongs and Evan asked me if I wanted one. So I said yes why not. I hadn't had one for a very long time. Evan and George [Evan's cousin from Greece] were saying how they were going to rape and kill me and dump me in the Port River. They did worry me a bit at first, so I just started playing along with them in a joking way. The next minute, out of the blue, Evan said, 'See you later George' and he jumped out [of the car] and left. I couldn't believe it.

When the passage was read out Evan said, 'It was just a joke. I hadn't known her very long. We were stoned and just mucking around. We were jabbering on, you know, talking shit, and George brought that up and I just went along with it, just to scare her, because we didn't know her very well at the time. Basically, my intention was to sleep with her, but she didn't turn out to be that type of girl. So it just came out, fake threats, to see her reaction.'

Counsel went on to suggest that Evan had been a bit too concerned about establishing an alibi after he discovered Shirree was murdered. Evan denied there was any substance to the accusation but admitted he knew the police would have questions. He knew he would need truthful answers, answers that could be checked out. His alibi proved to be solid.

Although some of the testimony revealed things I didn't know about my daughter's relationship with Evan I was enormously relieved that I had not been wrong about Evan as far as his alibi was concerned. He may have been extremely unwise in making those very foolish remarks to Shirree, but his distress at the news of Shirree's murder had been an honest reaction and not an act.

Chapter 9

What's Wrong with the Truth?

Detective Senior Sergeant Michael Johnson, who was appointed Administration Sergeant for the investigation, was the next witness to take the stand. Johnson was a typical cop and my first meeting with him had been less than ideal. I had given some advice to Fabio after the murder that had offended Johnson. Fabio spoke to me soon after the murder, swearing that he had nothing to do with Shirree's murder but worried what the police might be thinking. 'If you've got nothing to feel guilty about, then you've got nothing to worry about. If it's a problem, then you'd better get yourself a lawyer,' was my offending piece of advice.

When Johnson paid me a visit two weeks later it was not just to introduce himself to the father of a murder victim. He wanted to establish up-front that he did not appreciate me giving a suspect advice of any kind. Johnson made it very clear he would not tolerate any interference with the investigation. I apologised. Johnson's initially brusque manner softened and I found he was a man passionate about his work. Johnson had seen enough over his time in the force to harden any policeman's heart and seemed to understand what a victim's relatives went through.

Throughout the entire investigation and into the court proceedings I gained an appreciation of the frustration felt by law enforcers when their diligence and hard work seemed to be in vain and was treated with some disdain in the court system.

Detective Johnson's testimony revolved principally around the police investigation from the moment that Shirree's body was found and her death established as a major crime. Detective Johnson described in detail how the police inquiry into the murder was recorded within the police system:

> The system has the capability of storing recorded information, investigative procedures and results of inquiries from actions raised. All inquiries are recorded in this manner and each major crime has a separate identity in the computer. The Turner case was given identity number 93/20, indicating that it was the twentieth major crime declared since the beginning of the year [1993].
>
> It is an unfortunate but increasingly usual occurrence that pieces of false information having nothing to do with a crime are being received during most investigations. During this case police received and traced all of the calls from the emergency triple 0 number. Where possible, calls are followed up and all calls from public phone boxes or triple 0 calls are automatically traced to ascertain their origin. We received emergency triple 0 calls from public phones at the Adelaide Railway Station downtown, from the outer northern suburb of Salisbury and other areas.

The witness described one hoax call in detail to give the jury an idea of the type of false information police receive and are required to follow up.

One caller had stated his name and said that his son had returned the family car earlier in the afternoon on 9 June 1993. The caller stated that his son's name was the same as his. When he examined the car he found blood on a shirt and a vest belonging to his son. He also found a handkerchief with the initials ST in the boot. When a patrol car was dispatched to the address the officers were told that nobody of that name lived at the address nor did anybody have any knowledge of the phone call. Many such instances of false and misleading information were received and all were followed up. It was frustrating for police who had enough to do without the senseless stupidity of this type of mindless behaviour.

Detective Johnson stated that the Forensic Science Centre tested all knives handed in for blood and human tissue. If a negative result occurred they would either destroy them or return them to their owner. The knives belonging to Evan and Fabio were tested and eliminated as were the other knives handed in. The murder weapon was never found.

Tests are routinely made in cases of murder. Swab tests taken from the body and tape-lift tests from clothing look for fibres and other material. The Coroner found no DNA that would have linked Shirree with her killer. 'By the end of August 1993 all lines of inquiry were exhausted and all persons of interest interviewed and eliminated as suspects. The case had well and truly stalled and we could only wait for fresh information.'

Although the case was still open detectives were reassigned to other duties. Very little information was received for a period of two years. 'In August 1995 significant new information came in. We formed a new team. The new information led us to a group of men.'

Johnson said that Shane Cherry, a security guard at the Nightclub, was the last person to identify Shirree positively. There were also some doubtful sightings by persons who said they saw or spoke to a woman carrying three handbags. 'The police did not take many of these sightings seriously. Most were reported because of the publicity and there was no corroborating evidence given to warrant taking serious notice.'

Knives belonging to Evan and Fabio were of special interest. Johnson explained the procedure police follow regarding weapons seized in a murder investigation. 'If a negative result from forensic testing is achieved and there is no evidentiary value, the weapon is filed, placed in the property exhibits section or returned. Weapons can be destroyed at the discretion of police.'

Detective Johnson said none of the knives tested were of the type or dimension capable of inflicting the wounds suffered by the victim. All of the knives were tested for blood and human tissue and in each case produced a negative result. Evan's knife had been returned to him. Fabio's knife, the one used in the course of his employment as a pest controller, was also returned. However, police retained one of his fishing knives even though it proved too large to have been the murder weapon.

'Isn't it true that it was simply a matter of insufficient evidence for any charges to be laid that led to the elimination of certain suspects?' questioned Defence Counsel.

'I would say that the persons of interest, or the widely used term "suspects", were eliminated as a result of careful police investigation and statements from other people giving an alibi,' Johnson replied.

Defence Counsel was clearly unimpressed by the way police followed up some of the inquiries and Detective Johnson was forced to defend police procedures. Defence Counsel believed that it was not enough for police to state that 'in their opinion so-and-so was blowing his own bags', therefore inquiries into what so-and-so said or was heard to say were dropped on that basis.

Justice Mullighan, concerned that Counsel was dwelling too much on the police investigation, requested an explanation. Counsel said that she didn't care if the accusations were the truth or if they were figments of people's disordered imaginations. What she meant was that people were capable of making false statements and false confessions to the police. She claimed that the investigation was an example of the notoriety, 'the sort of big-noting and the sort of carry-on' that occurs in any investigation with a lot of publicity. Counsel was obviously confident and promised the reasons would become clear as the trial progressed.

The tactics of Defence Counsel did not impress me. I was confident Johnson could handle himself, but I could also see Mercuri's counsel was a powerful and clever attorney.

During Johnson's testimony I inadvertently discovered more information about Frank Mercuri's sordid past. The police were having difficulty producing a copy of a newspaper article depicting the photograph of Shirree used for most of the publicity. I offered the police one of my copies and a detective drove me home in an unmarked car to collect it. I had begun to hear rumours about Mercuri's history of violent crime so I spoke to the officer to see if he had any intimate knowledge about Mercuri's past.

I learned enough to cause an angry reaction and confronted Detective Johnson after his testimony. He had no choice but to tell me the truth about what police knew about Mercuri. I could not believe what I heard. The police and the Prosecutor had knowledge of Mercuri's propensity for violence, particularly against women, and the full story made my skin crawl.

When the police discovered Mercuri was in prison awaiting sentence, they were astonished to find he had been convicted of attempted rape and assault causing grievous bodily harm. And as if that wasn't bad enough, Mercuri's victim considered him a friend.

I sat in a stunned and angry silence in Detective Johnson's office during a break in the trial. 'Ken, I think you know that we discovered Mercuri was in jail after we got the tip-off from the informant. Naturally, we wanted to know why he was inside. We were in contact with the Victorian police about Shirree's murder. They sent us details of his previous arrests and convictions. We didn't want to tell you everything about Mercuri because what I'm going to tell you now is not a pretty story. You'll understand what I mean after you hear it.'

'On New Year's Eve 1994, the day after being released from prison for breaking parole conditions, Mercuri lured a woman friend to a motel room. He produced a knife and stabbed her several times because she resisted his sexual advances. He tried to rape her. She escaped and ran down a flight of stairs. He pursued her, caught her and dragged her up the stairs by her hair. He told her he was going to kill her and pushed her over the balcony railing to the car park below.

'As you can imagine, she was terrified. Badly wounded, she escaped again and was discovered by a passer-by and taken to hospital. She was treated and in time recovered physically and was able to testify in court,' Johnson explained.

I was sickened by what I heard and after digesting the impact of the story my contempt turned to disgust. 'Mick, what the hell are we dealing with here?'

'He's a bad one. His rap sheet is as long as my arm. He's been in and out of prison most of his adult life.' Johnson paused. 'I understand how you must feel, Ken. It pisses me off, too. We do our best to put these bastards away but the courts let them go. They get a slap on the wrist. They might do a token stretch in the can, but they're prepared for that. They know what to do; they know how to play the system.'

'Mick, I've got a bad feeling about this.'

'I don't blame you. How do you think the DPP feels? He's the one trying to prosecute the bastard. He's got him in court and can't use a lot of the shit we know about him.'

'Why? What's wrong with the truth?'

'Nothing's wrong with the truth. It's the law; the way the law works. You know, innocent until proven guilty.'

'You're not making me feel any better.'

'Sorry. Look, if his mates had kept their mouths shut we wouldn't know a thing about this bastard. We're lucky we know what we do.'

'It's a bit more than luck in my opinion,' I said.

'Call it whatever you like.' Johnson shrugged his shoulders.

'He had to have help. That's how he got away with it for so long.'

'Theoretically, you're right. I've had a few ideas about that. He didn't know too many people here so it doesn't take a genius to work out who might have been involved. But it's only suspicion. We can't prove a thing.'

'Paul's worried, isn't he? He doesn't think he can get a conviction.'

'He'll do what he can, Ken. He's a good prosecutor. Hang on to your hope. Don't give up, it's not over yet.'

'Thanks for telling me, Mick. I know you didn't want to, but at least I know why now. I just wish I knew why Shirree went with him.'

Johnson nodded. 'I'd like to know the answer to that, too.'

I couldn't help but think about what might have happened to Shirree allegedly in the hands of this man. Although Shirree did not know him, he took advantage of her vulnerability just as he had taken advantage of the other young woman who thought he was her 'friend'. Mercuri's 'friend' had known him for six years, during which time he'd never attempted to come on to her. If he could hurt a friend in such a manner then he would probably have no conscience about hurting a stranger.

Mercuri's intention, it seemed, was to satisfy his sexual appetite. When the young woman was attacked on New Year's Eve 1994 she resisted Mercuri's advances and as a result he became angry, pulling a knife and repeatedly stabbing her. He forced her to perform disgusting sexual acts. She fought bravely for her life and escaped, only to be pursued and caught again. After being tossed over the balcony the young woman continued to fight for her life. In terror she ran, bleeding and badly wounded, to a nearby park where she hid. A stranger discovered her cowering behind bushes, shaking with fear like a cornered animal.

Mercuri probably hoped she was dead but because of the attention the noisy attack caused he had to escape and hope he was home free. But she survived and he was now paying the penalty for what he'd done.

The police said Shirree fought bravely to stop the sexual attack on her. Her killer pulled a knife on her and repeatedly stabbed her. Did he think he had succeeded in killing her when he left her in the reserve? Did he try to make sure there was nothing that could connect him with murder before he left her for dead? How long did she lie in the reserve, mortally wounded and bleeding profusely, before she attempted to get help?

I could see little difference between what happened to the young woman on New Year's Eve 1994 and what happened to Shirree, except the other young woman survived and Shirree died. The facts were similar enough for me to be convinced the police had arrested the man who had committed Shirree's murder.

The information about Frank Mercuri's past criminal history should have been enough in my view to help the police and the prosecution to really nail this man. I asked Johnson if this information about Mercuri's criminal past could be used and he told me that it couldn't and the reasons why. Not happy with his explanation, I spoke to Paul Rofe.

I told Paul that I was furious about what I had learned and couldn't understand why the information could not be used in court. He explained that it was because every accused is given the presumption of innocence until proven guilty according to admissible evidence. The mere fact that an accused had already committed a similar crime didn't mean that he'd committed the crime for which he was currently being tried. The facts would have to be almost identical and in this case a lot more evidence would have to be unearthed to substantiate guilt beyond any reasonable doubt to even contemplate trying to use Mercuri's past criminal history and the Similar Fact Evidence Law.

Even after it was explained to me I still couldn't believe that the past criminal history of an accused couldn't be used in court, even if the history was similar in fact. I was repeatedly told that the case against Mercuri was weak and yet here was a piece of information that I felt should be heard in court. I could not understand why this man's propensity for violence could not be used to bolster the prosecution's case. I couldn't see how a jury could make a fair decision if the whole truth were not told. The law says that just because he has been convicted in the past, it doesn't mean he's guilty of the current charge. I could understand that anything not related to a current charge was irrelevent, but this man had a history of violence, particularly against woman. How was that irrelevant?

I was also told that leaking this information to the media, or outbursts of any kind, could cause a mistrial and other possible repercussions. I was strongly advised to drop any ideas along those lines if I was contemplating trying to bring it up. I was also strongly advised not to talk about what I now knew about Mercuri with anybody, at least until after the trial.

Paul Rofe said that if one of the witnesses brought up something then the prosecution could run with it even if the defence objected, but the chances of that happening were minuscule. After all, the only witnesses who might be privy to Mercuri's history during the trial were supposed to be his mates. I felt like an ant trying to push a barrow of cement uphill and had to bow to the expertise of those who knew the law better than I did.

The next witness was Shane Cherry. Cherry was a security guard employed by the Princes Berkeley Nightclub and knew Shirree. He had finished work for the night and was talking with one of his colleagues near the main entrance to the club. Shirree approached him and stopped to talk for a few minutes. Cherry stated the time was about 2.15 am.

Cherry offered to take Shirree home but she said that her 'friend' was going to take her. She gestured towards a man whom Cherry described as Italian looking, with longish hair and a medium to solid build. The man was standing about ten to fifteen feet away. Cherry noticed Shirree was carrying three handbags. It was obvious Shirree had been drinking but she was speaking clearly. She walked back to the waiting man and they headed toward Rundle Mall together.

Cherry said he'd never seen the man before although he'd only glanced at him once or twice. He was shown photographs by police and pointed to two of the photos as being similar to the man he saw with Shirree. He said neither of the men in the photographs was the man with her but both looked similar. Cherry pointed to a photograph of Fabio and another similar looking man who was in jail at the time of Shirree's murder.

Under cross-examination Cherry needed to clarify minor differences between his statement to police and his testimony in court. He agreed his recollection of what happened wasn't as clear as it was back in 1993. What was clear, however, was that Shane Cherry was probably the last person who knew Shirree to see her alive.

Dr John Gilbert, who conducted a post-mortem examination on Shirree's body, was called as the next witness. He gave details of his medical qualifications and experience and described the science of forensic pathology.

Dr Gilbert had been called to examine Shirree's body where she was discovered and described what he observed. He noted the state of Shirree's clothing and took the necessary steps to determine whether Shirree had been sexually assaulted. Tests to determine the approximate time of death were taken and he certified 'life extinct'.

At the morgue, Shirree's height and weight were measured and photographs of the whole procedure taken. Dr Gilbert described each stab wound, explaining some were defence wounds. There were nine stab wounds to the upper part of the body and one superficial cut to the left upper thigh. There were four major wounds to the chest.

Death was caused by a wound that penetrated the sac surrounding the heart, causing it to cease contracting. Other chest wounds contributed to massive blood loss but the wound to the heart was significant in regard to rapidity of death. Several bruises and abrasions were noted. Bruises on the knees were consistent with her falling heavily sometime during the trek from the park. Blood tests revealed a high alcohol content in her system and Dr Gilbert estimated time of death at approximately 4 am.

Since a murder weapon was never found, the effect of a knife penetrating a body lying down as opposed to a standing position was detailed. The type and dimension of knife capable of inflicting the wounds was considered and the expertise of the witness relied upon to determine the possible length, width and thickness of the blade.

Dr Gilbert said there was no unusual feature about the wounds and any number of commonly used knives could have been the murder weapon. He estimated the blade length at thirteen to fifteen centimetres, stating that a single-bladed knife caused the wounds.

Dr Gilbert was shown a knife. The length of the blade measured nine centimetres. The court heard that the knife exhibited could have inflicted the wounds provided some force was used. 'With compression of the chest by using force, the same result could be achieved with a blade length of nine to ten centimetres,' Dr Gilbert said. 'Many thousands of knives could have been the murder weapon. Most ordinary kitchen knives, which are usually used in stabbing cases, could have caused the injuries.'

Defence Counsel concentrated on two points. 'Would it be reasonable to expect that a longer bladed knife caused the wounds on the victim?' Counsel inquired.

'Yes. But a shorter blade, used with sufficient force, could inflict wounds of the nature found on the victim.'

While I was waiting outside the courtroom, Scott Schinella's father approached me. Mr Schinella introduced himself, extending his hand. He said he was very sorry about what happened to Shirree and his son's part in the scenario. He told me the police had visited his home in 1995 wanting to talk to his son about one of his son's friends. 'I had no idea that this friend was suspected of a murder.'

Mr Schinella said his son's conscience bothered him about lying to the police. Conscience and perhaps a little commonsense told him he was in trouble, and lots of it. Mr Schinella said that Scott had spoken to his girlfriend and her mother a few days after making his first statement to police. Scott was worried because in his first statement he hadn't told the whole truth. Schinella's girlfriend suggested he speak to his father who advised him to go back to the police and tell them what he knew.

The more I talked to Mr Schinella the more unreal the situation became. It was absurd to be making friendly small-talk with the father of one of the principal witnesses. Scott Schinella lied to protect himself, having little regard for what happened to my daughter at the hands of a gutless rapist and murderer, but, on the other hand I felt sorry for his father. His embarrassment about his son's actions seemed genuine.

We talked for a long time and although I still could not understand how Scott or any of the others could have no regard for Shirree or her family I respected Mr Schinella for his courage. I was learning a lot about the truth standing outside the court, but unfortunately the jury were not permitted to hear any of it.

Chapter 10

Unreliable Witnesses

The first of the prosecution's primary witnesses took the stand on 10 March in the second week of the trial. Scott Schinella told the court that he and a group of men from the Albert Street pool hall had known each other for many years, meeting at the pool hall three or four times each week. It was at the pool hall the he met Frank Mercuri, through his friends Julian Berti and Chris John Thallas.

Schinella stated that on the night of 5 June 1993 he and his girlfriend were out with several of her relatives. After taking his girlfriend home he was passing the Chambers Street apartment and noticed Julian Berti's car. Schinella stopped to visit. A few minutes later a vehicle drove into the driveway quickly, making a lot of noise.

Schinella testified that Mercuri entered the apartment extremely agitated, cursing and swearing, saying 'he had stabbed a girl'. He claimed Mercuri said, 'I was lying on some grass down the road with a girl and a man came along and began to kick into me. I got up and stabbed the man. The man ran off and I stabbed the girl.' Schinella said there were grass stains on Mercuri's jeans as if he had 'skidded across the grass'.

Shocked, scared and not wanting to have anything to do with the situation, Schinella left. He heard Mercuri ask Berti to drive him downtown and recognised the utility parked in the driveway as one of the vehicles from the petrol station.

Schinella drove home, went directly to bed and tried to forget what he heard. He later heard about the murder of a woman at Oaklands Park and put two and two together. He made no decision at the time about what to do with the information. Schinella said he ran into Mercuri outside the pool hall about two weeks later. Schinella said Mercuri asked him not to say anything about the murder and he agreed to keep quiet because he was afraid. Schinella alleged Mercuri repeated what he'd said that morning.

Schinella said he didn't see any of the group between 6 June and encountering Mercuri at the pool hall, except Julian Berti. He saw Berti about a week after the incident at the apartment.

Schinella was aware police were asking for assistance but he did not come forward because he was afraid for his personal safety. Schinella said the police eventually approached him. In the middle of September 1995 he gave police the first of three statements. His opinion of Mercuri was not flattering.

In his first statement to police Schinella had described Mercuri as 'the type of guy who had a mug mouth, a big mouth. He would try to talk louder than someone he was talking to. He would also big-note himself. He was the type that if something was insignificant he would make a big thing out of it. He was aggressive in how he talked to people. If someone bumped into him accidentally he would mouth off at them and would go on and on about it. He was a real hero boy. He had to be better than everyone else. He always thought he knew more about something than anyone else.'

Two weeks after his first statement Schinella told police he had initially lied and wanted to make a second statement, swearing it was the truth. His father and his girlfriend had advised him to tell the truth.

Schinella was easily rattled. Defence Counsel was relentless in cross-examination. Schinella didn't seem to understand what was being asked of him and his answers to Counsel's questions made less and less sense. Defence Counsel was amazed that there had been no discussion amongst the friends of the group about the murder. This was only eclipsed by her astonishment that no discussion had taken place between him and his best friend Thallas and Jacqueline Schilling after the first interview by the police.

Counsel insisted Schinella must have talked with Thallas about their situation. The witness denied it. Schinella also denied that Thallas had told him the police thought he (Thallas) might be 'an accessory after the fact' or that Thallas might have helped to 'clean up'. It was strongly suggested that the friends had talked and agreed to tell police a story to put Thallas out of the picture. Another denial.

Counsel continued to badger the witness. What Schinella said in his multiple statements and later at the committal hearing came back to haunt him. Counsel continued her relentless pursuit until the Prosecutor objected to the line of questioning. Justice Mullighan adjourned court until the next morning.

It was a pity that the man who Schinella said interrupted Mercuri with the girl could not be found. Police appealed for him to come forward and checked hospital emergency rooms for suspicious stabbing injuries from records of the time. No such man was ever found, giving little credence to Schinella's version of what Mercuri said happened. But if Schinella was telling the truth then Mercuri was lying, using this story to justify stabbing the girl.

✖

Schinella had all night to stew about what was going to happen when Defence Counsel resumed her vigorous cross-examination. She did not let him down. She was as dogged as she had been the previous day. Schinella still didn't seem to understand the questions. Counsel cleverly succeeded in confusing Schinella by moving from one issue to another rapidly. It was a brilliant cross-examination.

Counsel pushed the fact that it was inconceivable he would not talk to his friends, particularly Thallas, about the murder. Schinella had previously denied saying anything about the murder to anyone and was now saying an attack of conscience prompted him to discuss it with his girlfriend, her mother and his father.

On re-examination the Prosecutor tried to clarify what Schinella really knew and who he had discussed the situation with. It only proved to further hurt the prosecution case. 'Between the time you gave your first statement and the time you gave your second statement, you denied having spoken to Chris Thallas about this matter?' the Prosecutor asked.

'That's correct,' Schinella replied.

'Did you speak to any other person? Do you understand what I am talking about, the period?'

'No. What period?' Schinella queried.

'The period between giving the first statement to the police on 16 September and giving the second statement to them on 30 September—did you speak to any other person? By that I mean any other person outside of the group at the pool hall.' The Prosecutor could not have spelt it out any clearer.

'Concerning this matter?' Schinella queried.

'Yes,' the Prosecutor replied.

'No. I didn't.'

Whatever might have been left of Schinella's credibility crumbled down around the prosecution. What about the discussion he said he'd had with his father, his girlfriend and her mother? The conversation which, due to an attack of conscience, had instigated Schinella's visit to police to rectify the lies.

The Prosecutor's disappointment at the witness's response to the final question was not entirely unexpected. He had known going into the trial that the credibility of some witnesses and the stability of their character, their intelligence and lack of integrity were going cause problems. Schinella had clearly not understood the final question even though the Prosecutor spelt it out for him.

I didn't know it at the time but my conversation with Schinella's father had confirmed what Schinella said on the stand about talking the situation over with his father. But the Prosecutor knew nothing about my conversation with Mr Schinella and neither did the jury.

Schinella's ordeal was finally over. He was dismissed from the witness stand. Now the Prosecutor had an almost impossible task ahead of him and Defence Counsel must have been ecstatic. Schinella had played right into her hands.

Jacqueline Schilling was next to testify. She was the girlfriend of Chris John Thallas and when visited by police they were unaware she had information relevant to the inquiry. The Prosecutor established that in 1993 her social life revolved around occasional Saturday night outings because she worked afternoon shifts. She stated that she met Mercuri in Melbourne while she and Thallas visited a friend, Ricardo Berti. She said Thallas associated in the main with his cousin Chris George Thallas (Little Chris), Julian Berti, Scott Schinella and Mercuri.

Schilling saw Mercuri on a few occasions at the apartment, once at the pool hall and on a couple of occasions downtown. The witness explained that she was a 'night owl' and rarely arrived downtown before 10 pm. On the night in question she and Thallas saw Mercuri in Rosina Street, near the

Hindley Street end. Mercuri was with a woman who was leaning against a wall. Schilling hung back a little because she didn't want to talk to Mercuri at all. Thallas was well aware of her feelings about associating with Mercuri.

Schilling described the woman with Mercuri as 'in her early twenties with big boofy hair, dark blonde with highlights and a little below the shoulder in length. The hair was clipped up at the sides with combs or clips. She was wearing a black top and a dark coloured skirt and she noticed a cross or necklet of some kind at her throat.' She described the woman's make-up in some detail.

Thallas spoke to Mercuri for about five minutes. They left the downtown area at around 4 am and did not see Mercuri or the woman again. Defence Counsel asked for a description of Mercuri in 1993. 'He was bigger, more muscular and had more hair. The colour was the same. He had really short receding hair'. She guessed his age at about twenty-two years and seemed to remember a thin moustache. 'I can't recall if he always had the moustache but I remember he had one at some stage. I don't really follow fashion but Frank wore his hair shorter than most men.'

Schilling described the woman's clothing. She said the top was black but wasn't sure about the skirt because of the lighting. 'I imagine it was a dark colour because if it had been white or yellow it would have stood out as a lighter colour.

'The woman mumbled a lot but I didn't take notice of what she said. Nothing special stands out about that night except it was cold. I saw the publicity about the murder in newspapers but didn't immediately connect the photo with the woman I saw with Frank.

Schilling went on to say that she went with the police to Darlington and spoke with them for several hours. She said that other than saying how terrible it was, Chris had never spoken to her about the murder and Frank Mercuri in the same breath.

'Are you saying the first time you were asked to recall seeing Mercuri in the city with a woman was by the police?' the Prosecutor asked.

'Yes,' the witness replied.

Chris John Thallas was the next witness for the prosecution. He told the court he owned his own business, working as a motor mechanic, but prior to that he worked at a petrol station.

He associated with a group of young men who met regularly at a pool hall. Thallas became aware Mercuri had moved to Adelaide and was a regular visitor to the apartment. Thallas and Mercuri trained together using weights and be described their relationship as 'good'.

Mercuri was hired on a casual basis to do odd jobs, such as welding on the hire trailers at the petrol station where Thallas worked. The court heard Mercuri occasionally borrowed one of the utilities for private use.

There were times when they went out together and girls were included except on a boys' night out. Thallas and his girlfriend called in to Mercuri's apartment on the night in question for a few drinks and later saw Mercuri with a woman in Rosina Street.

Thallas's description of the woman was different from Schilling's and he was vague about details. The court heard that Thallas was about to walk past when Mercuri called to him. The woman was speaking a language Mercuri said he couldn't understand. Thallas told the court that it could have been Spanish or French. Thallas and Schilling continued walking toward Hindley Street. They did not see Mercuri again that night.

On the follwoing Monday, Mercuri came to the petrol station and appeared 'stressed out'. Mercuri said, 'I've done something stupid. I was lying in the bushes with a girl and some guy came along and started to hit me with a piece of wood or something. I turned around and stabbed him twice and he ran off. The girl was screaming so I turned around and stabbed her.'

Thallas said he didn't know whether to believe Mercuri or not but didn't want to hear any more and even after seeing a newspaper report didn't want to believe what he'd been told. The newspaper photograph was not clear enough for him to tell if the woman with Mercuri was the same woman, 'she just looked similar'.

'And did you speak to anyone else about what you allege you were told?'

'I wasn't talking about it,' Thallas said. 'It's not the sort of conversation you like to get into.'

'Please explain why you did not divulge what you knew,' the Prosecutor continued to probe.

'I was a bit scared of the situation. I was scared of what was going to happen. You know, courts, media and everything.'

The witness said he did not see much of Mercuri after the murder because Mercuri returned to Melbourne at the end of June. Their relationship changed a little after what Mercuri told him and he didn't want to have anything to do with the situation.

The court heard that Thallas gave Mercuri a birthday gift only a few days before the murder. Thallas told the court that a representative from the company Snap-on Tools visited the petrol station regularly. Thallas purchased tools for his trade as an apprentice mechanic from displays in the back of a van. Thallas showed his friend a range of knives and Mercuri said he wouldn't mind one of them. Since his friend's birthday was not far away Thallas made the decision to purchase a knife for him.

The knife Thallas gave Mercuri was similar in colour and design to the single-bladed knife already admitted into evidence. At the time he purchased the birthday knife for Mercuri he also purchased a knife for himself. The court heard how Thallas was known to go goat shooting occasionally and had bought other knives from the same company. The Prosecutor produced receipts.

Soon after Thallas opened his own business he hired a utility for Mercuri, who had come back to Adelaide with the intention of returning to Melbourne with his possessions. Thallas denied he knew that Mercuri wanted to take the vehicle to Melbourne. When the utility was not returned Thallas became worried. Several days later he received a call. Mercuri said he used the vehicle to transport his belongings to Melbourne and was in hospital and unable to return the vehicle. Thallas was furious, reported the utility stolen, eventually having to pay $800 to recover the vehicle. He admitted he was upset about having to pay the recovery costs.

Thallas stated he would never have told the police what Mercuri told him but they came to him two years later and he had no choice. Court was due for a break and the Prosecutor applied for the representative from Snap-on Tools to be called to give evidence interposed into Thallas's testimony. The application was granted. The court was not finished with Thallas but he was stood down to allow for testimony to confirm the purchase of two knives just before the murder.

Stephen Ponting was an authorised dealer for Snap-on Tools and drove a van to various destinations to sell tools and other items. The van was like a shop on wheels and Thallas was a client, operating an account. He identified three receipts issued on 2 June 1993. Thallas paid an amount which was deducted from his account and recorded on the first receipt. The balance owing on his account was also shown on the receipt.

The second receipt related to the sale of a knife, part number KER 1320, which was inscribed on the blade. It was an Italian-manufactured single-bladed knife. The witness recalled a conversation he had with Thallas about the knife. Thallas wanted to buy a birthday present for a friend and asked for something special, a bit out of the ordinary. The knife he purchased was considered a bit out of the ordinary because it was handmade from Italy and therefore a little more expensive than the other Japanese knives. Thallas purchased the knife, asking that it be charged to his account.

The third receipt also related to the sale of a knife to Thallas but this knife was paid for with cash. It was described as a diving knife. This knife was double-edged, and clipped onto a belt. Thallas wanted this knife for himself.

On cross-examination the witness explained Thallas needed receipts for the tools he purchased for taxation purposes. Defence Counsel suggested Thallas might have bought the knife on the cash receipt, the double-bladed diving knife, as the birthday gift.

Ponting was quite certain Thallas had indicated he intended to give the first knife, the Italian single-bladed knife, as the gift because he wanted something special. However he conceded the second knife, the one paid for with cash, pointed to a personal purchase. Mercuri was not present when the knives were purchased.

Following Ponting's testimony Thallas prepared to resume his place on the witness stand. He could not have been expecting anything other than a torrid time. Defence Counsel was relentless. Of special interest was the fact that Thallas did not discuss what he alleged Mercuri confessed to him with anyone, not even his girlfriend. He said Jacqueline had remarked that the woman depicted in the newspapers looked remarkably similar to the woman who was with Mercuri, but he continued to deny he discussed the situation with her fully before police interviewed them in September 1995.

Thallas looked rattled but the Defence took no pity. He showed almost the same degree of confusion as his friend Schinella. The brilliance of the Defence Counsel shone through as she fired question after question at the witness. It was obvious Thallas had decided he was only going to say exactly what he needed to say to get out of trouble. He did not seem to be concerned that much of his testimony made little sense.

Counsel queried the timing of the confession compared with his girlfriend's first comment on the newspaper article. 'I just kept it between my girlfriend and me because she put one and one together,' Thallas said. He repeated that he had not spoken about the confession with Jacqueline initially but said that if it had been recorded in the police interview then he probably hadn't understood the question. 'When Jacqui brought the subject up I just brushed it off.'

The witness could not explain what the 'it' was that was being kept between himself and his girlfriend. He finally admitted that they discussed some things before 16 September when the police came but continued to deny he told her about the confession.

Defence Counsel did her best to confuse Thallas. She suggested that he gave the double-edged diving knife to Mercuri and kept the other single-bladed Italian knife for himself, but when Thallas was shown the single-bladed knife admitted into evidence he stated, 'That looks like the knife I gave to Frank.'

Thallas explained that he went goat shooting and that was why he purchased a knife for his personal use. It made more sense to the police and me that the double-edged knife with a clip-on pouch would be more useful to Thallas on his shooting expeditions.

Counsel repeatedly raised what Thallas said to police in his interview, what he signed in his statement and what he testified at the committal hearing. Thallas said when police came to his business telling him they wished to interview him in relation to Frank Mercuri and the Shirree Turner murder he told them he didn't know what they were talking about.

At Police Headquarters where his interview was videotaped he realised he couldn't continue to hide what he knew. He said he pretended nothing had happened after the confession and kept seeing Mercuri. During the interview police asked if he was implicated in the murder.

'It must have been quite a shock to you to have these type of questions put to you,' Counsel probed.

Thallas agreed and said it was some time later when he became aware that Schinella and other members of the group were interviewed on the same day. He admitted that some of the group spoke to him later about their interviews. Most of the group was scared after the initial police operation and did not see one another for a long time.

Defence Counsel suggested that police accused Thallas of being involved, 'helping to clean up' after the crime. Thallas said he couldn't recall being specifically asked the question but was worried the police didn't believe he was not involved. Thallas said he hadn't seen Schinella after the day police came to the workshop except at Schinella's wedding. Schinella had admitted he was 'really stressed out' after the police came, but Thallas insisted they hardly saw one another.

Defence Counsel accused Thallas of spreading malicious gossip and trying to big-note himself. It was suggested that the police were trying to prove Thallas was implicated in some way and that he had been shooting his mouth off around town. It was further suggested that Thallas and Schinella had concocted a story to back Thallas's version of the events. 'No! No! That's not right. We weren't seeing much of each other. We kind of drifted apart,' Thallas claimed.

Defence Counsel suggested that when Thallas hired the utility he knew that Mercuri intended to take his possessions back to Melbourne. It was further suggested that a green Valiant belonging to Mercuri was left in an undriveable condition by members of the group and that some of Mercuri's possessions had gone missing or were trashed while he was in Melbourne. Defence Counsel further alleged that some of the group were not happy about being accused of trashing Mercuri's things and an argument had developed thus leading to the group drifting apart.

Defence Counsel claimed Thallas knew Mercuri was upset with the group and agreed that Mercuri could take the utility to Melbourne. It was further claimed Thallas himself had something to do with the trashing of the Valiant and other possessions belonging to Mercuri and that there was a good deal of ill-feeling between them all. Thallas claimed, 'I had my own business to run. I didn't have time to run around wrecking cars or anything else.'

Thallas denied he knew Mercuri was taking the utility to Melbourne. 'He promised to pay for the costs,' Thallas said. 'My business was just getting started. I couldn't afford to pay the money to get the utility back but I had to. He never paid me back.'

Defence Counsel was amazed that no significant interaction occurred about such an important event. 'I suggest to you that you brought it down on your own head by what you had spread around and then you found yourself being asked by police officers whether you were involved in a murder.' Thallas said he was shocked the police were questioning him about being implicated and denied it was because he'd spread malicious gossip.

'I didn't say nothing to no-one,' Thallas replied.

Defence Counsel completed cross-examination of the witness and Thallas was released from the witness box.

Detective Bill Cunningham and Detective Craig Spencer both told the court how they had travelled to the Melbourne jail where Mercuri was being held on 14 October 1995. Mercuri declined to be interviewed. Detective Spencer cautioned Mercuri, advising him that he was not obliged to answer questions unless he wished to do so, but anything he did say would be taken down and given in evidence.

Again Mercuri declined. He was asked if he wished to be informed of the allegation and declined for a third time. Mercuri gave his full name and date of birth but little else. He was arrested after speaking with his solicitor.

'After the interview with Chris John Thallas investigators checked crime reports for a stabbing assault around the time of the murder. If a person attends a casualty section of a public hospital with suspicious injuries, such as stab wounds or bullet wounds, the hospital will automatically notify police. There were no reports of a stabbing assault anywhere near the time of this murder.'

'We have no more witnesses to call, Your Honour. That completes the case for the Crown,' Rofe announced.

Defence Counsel raised the issue of the prosecution's reluctance to call a certain witness, Julian Berti, to testify. Their worry was that Berti had been established as a material witness but he wasn't being called to testify simply because of contradictory statements relating to Schinella's evidence, even though there was no conflict of interest about who was present on the night in question.

The Prosecutor conceded he should call Berti and formally requested an adjournment. Julian Berti was always reluctant to speak with police and there had been difficulty locating him at times. It remained to be seen if the police would succeed in locating the witness this time.

My friends and I took the opportunity to leave the vicinity of the court for a coffee break. My expectation about the outcome of the trial was not encouraged when I was told that Julian Berti was being sought to testify. I doubted Berti would have an attack of conscience. In fact, it was felt all round that the testimony of Julian Berti would probably be the final nail in the coffin for the prosecution team.

After Julian Berti had been located I knew the Prosecutor wasn't expecting any pleasant surprises. Berti was expected to testify just as he had at the committal hearing. The prosecution team and police were convinced he was avoiding the truth and he knew more than he was prepared to tell, even under oath.

Julian Berti told the court he met Frank Mercuri at his brother's twenty-first birthday celebration. What the court did not hear was that Berti's brother was in jail with Mercuri at the time. Sometime after the birthday celebration Berti's brother asked him to 'look after Frank' when he came to Adelaide early in 1993. Berti said Mercuri stayed with his family for several weeks.

Berti's mother helped Mercuri find the apartment and set him up with furniture, crockery, cutlery and linen. Julian Berti signed the lease for Mercuri although he didn't actually live there. He stayed overnight on occasions and used the apartment as a drop-in centre, just as the other members of the group did.

Berti knew about the relationship between Mercuri and Thallas. The activities of the group were centred mainly at the apartment where they held parties and drinking sessions. They also went to the Albert Street pool hall, Hindley Street nightclubs and other venues on occasions. Berti spent a lot of time at the apartment drinking heavily when he was 'unemployed and had no real commitments'.

The Prosecutor examined the witness about the night of 5 June and the early hours of 6 June 1993. There were no surprises. He told the same story as at the committal hearing although the Prosecutor had the impression he was trying to tone the story down.

In his interview with the police the description of Mercuri's state of mind was quite different from the description he was giving now. Berti stated at the committal hearing that Mercuri was annoying him with his cursing and swearing and agitated attitude and he had told him to 'shut up and leave him alone'. Berti said that when Mercuri came home he was acting a bit unusual. 'He was hyperactive and swearing, like he was really upset about something. He came in quite agitated, more than usual.'

The prosecutor had then asked him, 'Describe what you mean by the term "hyperactive"?'

'He was walking around talking to himself, swearing, rambling,' Berti had said. 'He was saying "f... this, and f... that". I wasn't really paying much attention to it. I don't remember him swinging his arms around. I just told him to shut up and leave me alone, stop annoying me. He was too noisy for me the way he was going on. I just wanted some peace and quiet.'

Now, Berti was saying Mercuri was a 'bit hyperactive' and 'nothing major really happened'. According to Berti, Mercuri 'walked around swearing a bit and was rather annoyed'. He said Schinella stayed for a short time and a little later, after Mercuri settled down, he and Mercuri headed downtown. Berti couldn't recall how they travelled or which route they had taken.

Under cross-examination Berti denied hearing Mercuri say anything about stabbing a girl and even though he was drinking heavily he thought he would remember if such a conversation took place.

The court heard that Berti never saw Mercuri carrying a knife, nor was he aware Thallas had given Mercuri a knife for his birthday. He was never asked for a plastic bag to put handbags in and he never saw Mercuri with three handbags in the apartment. He did not deny driving Mercuri downtown but said if he had, it would have been a safer option to drive via back streets rather than the main road, to avoid breathalysers.

Berti knew about the incident regarding the hired utility. He helped Mercuri store some of his belongings, including a car, in a shed leased in Lonsdale. He denied knowing about any ill-feeling or dispute between Mercuri and the rest of the group over trashing Mercuri's car and other things. There was no re-examination by the Prosecutor.

Chapter 11

The Accused

An accused is not required to testify. However, Frank Mercuri chose to do so. As I was no longer required as a witness I was able to hear every word of his testimony.

The court heard that since his arrest for Shirree's murder Mercuri had been in a state of depression and the medication he was taking 'delayed' his reactions. Mercuri confirmed his previous testimony about his arrival in Adelaide early in 1993, his stay with the Berti family until he moved into the apartment and his association with the members of the group. He said he spent more time with Chris John Thallas than any other members of the group and confirmed the group's activities. He also confirmed details of casual employment at the petrol station and that he used a vehicle for personal use on a couple of occasions.

Mercuri recalled borrowing a vehicle overnight and travelling to Victoria to visit his brother. When he got back to Adelaide Thallas gave him a birthday gift. He described the gift as a double-edged knife in a pouch, which clipped to a belt. He said he did not ask for the knife but accepted it to be polite.

Mercuri could not remember what he did on 5 June 1993. 'It was too long ago,' he said. He had no specific memory about being with a woman in Rosina Street but did not dispute that he might have at some time.

The accused became aware of the allegation of murder when police came to arrest him. 'They accused me of all sorts of things. I just wanted to speak to my solicitor.' He said he'd tried hard to remember what he'd done in June 1993 but hadn't had any success in recalling anything. He didn't have any specific memory about returning to the apartment in an agitated state when Berti and Schinella were present. 'There were always people staying over at the apartment.' He couldn't recall the specific time Berti testified about. The only time he could recall being agitated was when he discovered his possessions had been trashed.

Mercuri denied having any conversation about a murder with Schinella and Berti. He denied any conversation between him and Schinella outside the pool hall and denied asking Schinella to keep quiet about a conversation at the apartment. And he denied having the same conversation with Thallas at the petrol station.

Mercuri moved to Melbourne in August 1993 after a quick trip back to Adelaide. Before he moved to Victoria he stored his belongings in a shed leased by Julian Berti, returning early in 1994 to find his belongings had been 'trashed'. Mercuri blamed the group and argued with Thallas who, according to Mercuri, took responsibility for the entire group and apologised for the damage. 'I held him totally responsible,' Mercuri said.

Mercuri admitted Thallas hired a utility for him to take his things back to Victoria and that his intention was to return to Adelaide, repair the green Valiant and drive it back. However, he'd been involved in an accident and admitted into hospital overnight. He phoned Thallas, said he could not return the vehicle because he had damaged his shoulder, told Thallas where the vehicle was parked and promised to repay the recovery costs. Mercuri admitted he never reimbursed Thallas and said they had not spoken since.

'Have you ever met a woman by the name of Shirree Turner?'

'No, I haven't.'

'Did you have anything to do with the murder of Shirree Turner?'

'No, I did not.' No surprises. Defence Counsel concluded the examination and invited the Prosecutor to cross-examine.

'Please tell the court where the knife is currently,' Rofe questioned Mercuri.

'I imagine it's still with my things.' He said he stored a lounge suite, refrigerator and some bits and pieces to furnish an apartment in a shed. Thallas's cousin (Little Chris) helped to transport them in his van before Mercuri returned to Victoria to find work. He said he had a plastering job lined up in Melbourne and hadn't driven the green Valiant, which he originally bought from Little Chris, because he hadn't been able to afford to register the car and wasn't sure if it was mechanically sound at the time.

The accused said he was surprised when Thallas gave him a knife. He couldn't tell how much it was worth but thanked Thallas and put it in the bedroom cabinet. Mercuri denied he carried the knife around with him and denied it was the same as the knife already introduced into evidence.

The Prosecutor pressed Mercuri into describing the knife. 'I didn't have much to do with it,' was the reply. 'It was a double-bladed knife and it was a dark colour. I think the handle was a bit different to a normal handle and it had its own pouch.'

'After you put it away in your bedroom did you use it on any occasion after you were given it?' the Prosecutor asked.

'No. I don't use knives,' Mercuri replied. He assumed Thallas knew he didn't use knives and was surprised when given the knife for his birthday. He didn't tell Thallas he was not in the habit of using knives but accepted the gift because he 'didn't want to appear rude'.

'It is also quite fortunate for you that you cannot produce the knife, isn't it?' the Prosecutor continued.

'I can't tell you where my things are. I haven't spoken to Julian about them.'

The accused became exasperated at having to repeat himself concerning the details about the hired utility. He insisted Thallas knew he was taking the vehicle to Victoria with the things that were not trashed. It was part of the argument he'd had with Thallas about how he was supposed to get his things back to Victoria since he held the group responsible for trashing them. He said Thallas was very angry that he wasn't able to bring the vehicle back.

'Irrespective of this incident in early 1994, and prior to 1993 when you were living in the apartment, he [Thallas] was the person in the group you spent the most time with?' the Prosecutor probed.

'No. We only trained together and I worked a bit with him. It's not like I spent more time with him,' Mercuri replied.

The Prosecutor pressed the issue. Earlier in his testimony Mercuri stated he'd spent more time with Thallas than the rest of the group. So why was he trying to distance himself from the friendship now? Most of the group who were interviewed or testified in court agreed that Mercuri spent more time with Thallas than with any of the others.

'I didn't really know him [Thallas] that well. I didn't know the whole group that well.' It was obvious Mercuri was attempting to distance himself from the group. Why?

Mercuri didn't have any relations in Adelaide and he only associated with the group. He hadn't formed any long-term relationship with a woman either, admitting to one-night stands on occasions.

Mercuri said he didn't make a habit of using vehicles from the petrol station overnight, remembering only two occasions. The first was work related and the second was for the birthday trip in 1993 when he drove to Melbourne to visit his brother.

Mercuri's memory about the weekend following the trip to Melbourne was hazy. The group often met at the apartment and drank before a night out so he could not recall whether they had specifically done so that weekend. He couldn't recall leaving Berti at the apartment, nor could he remember coming home to find Berti and Schinella there.

Mercuri directly contradicted Detective Cunningham's testimony about his arrest. He said the detectives accused him of all sorts of things, telling him they were arresting him for murder, and all he wanted to do was speak to his solicitor. It was highly unlikely the police would blow their chances of an arrest by improper procedures questioning a suspect over a matter as serious as murder.

It was convenient that his memory was so bad he could not recall anything he did at the weekend. His memory was pretty clear about going to Melbourne to visit his brother and about receiving the knife from Thallas as a birthday gift. He'd given a reasonable description for someone who 'doesn't use knives', placing it in a bedroom cabinet after a cursory glance so as 'not to appear rude'.

The accused stated he didn't know where the knife ended up. He assumed it was with the rest of his belongings but didn't know what had happened to the rest of his 'trashed' possessions. Wasn't it obvious the trashed possessions would have been quickly disposed of? Why would anyone keep worthless trashed property for over four years?

Justice Mullighan adjourned court. Mercuri's cross-examination would be completed the next day. After final addresses by opposing counsels and the summing up of the evidence by the Judge, the jury would retire to consider their verdict. I didn't envy them. I was feeling more than a little nervous about their decision.

The next day the jury asked for Mercuri to be directed to speak in a louder voice because they'd had some difficulty hearing him the previous day. Mercuri said he'd stopped taking his medication because he couldn't concentrate. Prosecuting Counsel asked him to explain if side effects of the medication might affect his ability to remember details. It was established the medication did not cause memory lapses.

Whatever questions the Prosecutor asked about the murder, Mercuri's response was vague. His standard answers were 'I don't remember' or 'It's possible'. On all other issues his memory was clear. Mercuri did his best to make the group look really bad about their attitude toward him. He said they used him and took over the apartment.

The Prosecutor probed around every detail of Mercuri's examination by the Defence. He said he'd never been in Oaklands Reserve, never met or heard of Shirree Turner until police accused him of her murder and even though it had occurred close to the apartment he said he could not recall anything about it. He denied any conversation with members of the group regarding the murder.

The only events that stood out in Mercuri's memory were birthdays, 'because he could remember every birthday', and the day he was accused and charged with murder; 'I'll never forget that day'. He would never forget the day he was given a knife. It was the first time he'd ever been given a knife as a gift. These were significant days in the life of the accused.

He strongly denied the birthday gift was the same as the knife shown as an exhibit and agreed the knife Thallas gave him could not have been the murder weapon. 'I don't know what it was worth,' he said in answer to the Prosecutor's question, 'I don't have anything to do with knives.'

When Mercuri returned to Adelaide to collect his things he didn't let anyone know he was coming. He contacted Thallas on arrival to try to locate 'Little Chris', who was unavailable. Thallas drove Mercuri to the shed where they found his things trashed. Mercuri said Thallas apologised on behalf of the group for the damage and after an argument offered to hire the utility for him. Undamaged items were taken to an apartment belonging to Ricardo Berti where he packed his clothing and left for Melbourne.

Mercuri stated it was his intention to bring the vehicle back to Adelaide but he was involved in a car accident in Melbourne and couldn't drive because he damaged his shoulder. He'd moved the utility away from where he was staying because he didn't want to run into Thallas. Nor did he want Thallas to know where he was living.

The Prosecutor raised the fact that during the time Mercuri stayed at Ricardo Berti's apartment every one of the group except Schinella visited him. Mercuri said it was the new meeting place for the group. It was interesting that the only member of the group who did not visit during this time was Schinella. Mercuri said the last time he saw Schinella was in 1993 and their relationship was not very friendly. 'It's fair to say they don't like me and I don't like them,' he said.

Mercuri seemed to be distancing himself from the group again and justified his statement by saying they used him because of the apartment and when he began to see them for their 'true colours' he simply left town. Mercuri was reminded that just a few weeks prior to leaving Adelaide he'd been given a rather expensive birthday present. 'Isn't it a little strange, if the relationship between you and the group was so strained, that Thallas would give you such a birthday gift since you had only known each other for a few months? Why would he give you such an expensive gift.'

Mercuri stuck with his story that the birthday present and hiring of the utility was not a gesture of friendship but a peace offering because of the way the group treated him and for 'using and abusing the apartment'.

'Do you recall being in Rosina Street with a woman when Thallas and his girlfriend spoke to you?'

'It's possible.'

'Did you ever take a woman to Oaklands Reserve?'

'Never.'

'Shirree Turner?'

'Never.'

Defence Counsel had no questions on re-examination. The accused returned to the dock. There were no more witnesses. Justice Mullighan and both attorneys agreed that since closing addresses and summing up of the evidence would take some time, the Judge should address the jury:

What remains in the trial is the very important addresses of counsel and the summing up I will give before you will be asked to retire. It would be undesirable for a weekend to separate closing arguments, the summing up and your very important deliberations. There should be a flow-on from one stage to the next. I propose to adjourn now and resume the trial on Monday when you will hear the addresses of counsel, my summing up and maybe on Monday or perhaps Tuesday you will be asked to retire and consider your verdict.

The jury left the court and Justice Mullighan, Defence Counsel and the Prosecutor discussed concerns about some of the evidence. Jacqueline Schilling's testimony regarding who she thought the woman was with Mercuri in Rosina Street was the prime concern for the defence.

The Prosecutor and Justice Mullighan were concerned about the heavy emphasis placed on Detective Johnson's testimony regarding the investigation into the number of calls received about confessions and overheard conversations about the murder. The defence inference that police didn't follow up enough needed an explanation. Court was adjourned and it remained to be seen what would eventually be made of these issues when court resumed after the weekend.

I was happy to have time away from court. Exhaustion was a constant companion and I was exasperated by sitting around the courts trying to concentrate and getting very little sleep. Trying to remain positive under the circumstances was an additional pressure. My 'I must remain strong' attitude didn't help, although I knew I would be angry with myself if I folded now.

I hadn't thought too much about what would happen after the trial. If the jury decided Mercuri was guilty, would it bring closure to this part of my life? Would I feel vindicated? I doubted it. So, how was I going to face the rest of my life? Would the nightmares miraculously cease when it was over? Whatever happened in the next few days was going to affect me for the rest of my life. My health problems were not going to disappear because of a conviction and sentence. I was still going to have to find a way to deal with life without my daughter whatever the verdict was.

When I thought about the possibility of a 'not guilty' verdict my mind wanted to shut down completely. I could not comprehend how I would cope with that. I tried to remain impartial in my thinking toward Mercuri. But the more I heard during the trial and the more I discovered about his character the more convinced I was of Mercuri's guilt.

Was it possible the jury would deliver a 'not guilty' verdict? According to the Prosecutor it was more than a possibility. It would not be long. A few more days and my life would take on a new direction, a direction dependant on the decision of twelve ordinary people. I had to prepare for both possibilities. I did not want to be caught unprepared for either eventuality.

A victim impact statement was prepared with help from the family, my doctor and a legal advisor, even though there was a distinct possibility I would never have an opportunity to deliver the statement. Paul Rofe and Detective Johnson, although hoping for a miracle, were not confident that the jury could convict on the evidence presented. Our chance of success had diminished because the credibility and character of some of the witnesses was in question and what was known about the past of the accused was inadmissible.

I tried to empty my mind over the weekend but found it was impossible. Since I could not turn off my thoughts I let them flow. I'd tried this approach before and had some success gaining a different perspective. I visited my daughter's grave over the weekend. I wanted to spend some time quietly reflecting on Shirree herself, not the murder. In the past I had found a sense of peace for a short time after visiting her grave and I was hoping to find a little of that peace again. None came. The past two weeks had drained me more than I was prepared to admit.

I wondered how much fight I had left. The biggest crisis in my life had taught me to be courageous, but I sometimes felt the newfound courage deserted me. I needed an injection, a booster shot. Standing in front of the headstone I reflected on the past five years. 'You weren't supposed to die before me,' I thought.

I felt the anger. In unguarded moments my dark side wanted to take over. The natural response to my daughter's death included thoughts of retribution. I tried to suppress the angry thoughts because I knew they were wrong and dwelling on them would only hurt me more.

It amazed me how many people thought about revenge and I was astounded at the variety of creative punishments that people came up with. Few understood why I'd forgiven Shirree's killer. Many friends, and even family, queried my sanity in forgiving a murderer. Even my doctor questioned my reasons. Dr Williams was fascinated at my insistence that I had to forgive. She told me she'd read and heard a lot about the result of holding on to unforgiveness and in her practice she was aware that a good majority of her patients were adversely affected by anger, bitterness and resentment.

There was no optimistic prognosis for the recovery of my health. Obviously I would never be able to forget about Shirree and the matters surrounding her death. It was not possible to let go. But maybe, just maybe, there was a way to deal with it.

Was it possible to turn the tragedy into something else? I started to think there might be a way to use the difficulty to do something positive rather than dwell on the negatives. It would take a huge amount of courage and determination but it was not the first time the thoughts had entered my mind. When I was in Queensland I thought about talking to youth groups and high school kids about personal safety issues, using Shirree's experience as a guide. It would require much thought and planning and for now I didn't have the strength; again I put the idea on the back burner.

I felt better for having visited the grave. It was not the first time I'd felt Shirree's approval for something I was thinking about. When I moved to Queensland I felt she approved of the move and now I felt that she approved of my thoughts about turning the tragedy of her murder into something more positive. I'd arrived at the gravesite feeling lonely and depressed. Now, as I was preparing to leave I felt comforted. I wasn't a victim. I was a survivor and I was determined to survive this. I didn't know how I was going to do it but I had to remain strong for Shirree. Only a few more days to go.

Chapter 12

Innocent?

The role of both counsels in closing was to present the evidence, test the evidence and assist the jury to look at the evidence. Had the prosecution proved beyond reasonable doubt that the accused murdered Shirree? It was the question in everyone's mind.

Paul Rofe was straight down the line summing up. He admitted upfront that it was an unusual and difficult case, the principal reason being it had taken nearly five years to bring the events of 6 June 1993 into court. The long delay caused difficulties of memory recall, detail, times and sequence of events. Rofe reminded the jury about the time frame given by Dr Gilbert, certain details about the kind of knife used in the attack, intoxication of the victim, last sightings by people known to Shirree and the discovery of the body and the handbags were all indisputable facts.

Rofe explained that the accused had denied murdering Shirree and didn't have any memory about what he was doing on 5–6 June 1993, although he clearly remembered the birthday trip to Melbourne and being given a knife as a gift.

Rofe claimed that there was absolutely no reason for Thallas and Schinella to fabricate such a ridiculous story about an innocent man and encouraged the jury to focus only on the evidence in their deliberations at the end of the Judge's summing up. He believed that the criticisms made by the Defence about the way police handled the investigation was not evidence and that the jury should be aware that some of the testimony was given only to complete a picture. Rofe also discussed the fact that the two main witesses, Schinella and Thallas, had both given important evidence that Mercuri had actually admitted to the crime.

> The case, the prosecution case, rests entirely on the evidence of Thallas and Schinella, what the accused told them.
>
> To convict the accused you must accept those critical parts of their evidence beyond resonable doubt in two ways; both as to the fact, that is the accused did, in fact, say it to them, and also as to the truth, namely not only did he say it to them but what he told them was, in fact, the truth.

Rofe went on to say that the Defence had suggested Thallas was circulating vicious gossip about the accused and when confronted by police Thallas feared they might accuse him of being more involved and so he recruited Schinella, convincing him to change his story to back Thallas up. Rofe told the jury that he thought this raised a number of questions. Was Thallas spreading malicious gossip? Was he angry about the utility incident? If the story was concocted then it was a bit of an elaborate story to be made up over $700 or $800. And why Schinella? Why wouldn't he have Schilling or Berti back him up? Why would Schinella agree to invent such a dangerous story? And why involve Berti? Rofe suggested that any way you looked at the so-called concocted story it was a gigantic lie. In anticipation of what Defence would ineviatably say about the two main witnesses, Rofe was honest with the jurors.

People lie. There is no question about that. We know that. It is an ordinary human experience ... You have seen them, that is Schinella and Thallas, and you have heard them. It is important that you assess them in terms of their intelligence, their command of the language, their demeanor and so on. Always bear in mind that they themselves, are far from totally creditable. If they are telling you the truth, for more than two years they sat on this information, despite the requests from the police for help, the requests from the family for help. Not until they were confronted by police did it come to light. They deserve criticism for that, no question about it.

Rofe again posed a question to the jury. Wouldn't it be more surprising if there were not some inconsistencies in their stories given the time factor? But why would they lie? Why would they implicate Mercuri?

The Prosecutor walked the jury through the more probable sightings of Shirree. Special attention was focused on persons who knew her. Each piece of evidence was given due consideration as the prosecution pieced together what it could about Shirree's murder. Details of the evidence from the crime scene suggested Shirree was lying on her back when attacked, as seen by the dirt and debris on her jacket and skirt. The direction of the stab wounds also suggested that Shirree was attacked while lying on the grass beneath a tree. The ripped underwear and the cut up the centre of the skirt together with a knife cut on one of her legs indicated that a sexual assault occurred although no semen was found from swab tests.

As part of his summation Rofe continued to elaborate on specific parts of the investigation. He told the jury that Shirree's wounds indicated the type of knife used was a single-bladed weapon similar to any number of knives found in any home. Thallas had given the accused a knife for his birthday only a couple of days before the murder, a knife which could have been responsible for the wounds inflicted. Since the actual murder weapon was never found, an identical knife to the one Thallas said he gave the accused was admitted into evidence. The evidence of both Thallas and Ponting pointed to the fact that this was the type of knife given as the birthday gift but the accused had vigorously denied this. He had said he received the double-bladed knife as the birthday gift.

The Prosecutor told the jury the most significant feature of evidence about the knife came from the accused himself. The accused's evidence generally stated that it was five years ago, he didn't do it, he didn't remember. But he was certain about one thing. He was given the double-bladed knife. Why? Because a double-bladed knife could not have caused the injuries. This certainty came from someone who was not into knives, was very surprised when Thallas came up with a knife as a birthday gift and after accepting the knife so as not to appear rude, threw it into the bedroom drawer. According to the accused, he never took it out, never showed it to anyone, never used it. Then, of course, the knife mysteriously disappeared with Mercuri's trashed belongings after he'd dumped it with the rest of his possessions in a shed leased by Julian Berti.

The prosecution reviewed the critical evidence of Schinella, Thallas, Berti and the accused:

> *After a sexual assault that you might think, because we found no semen, was interrupted for some reason, [Shirree was] stabbed. Whether by the intervention of another person, or by her own struggles, that culminated in the stabbing, after the clothes had been cut, whatever. The stabbing occurred. The accused returned to his flat. Schinella and Berti are there. The prosecution say he said what he said, according to Schinella. But, Schinella left almost immediately …*

Rofe went on to say that Berti then drove the accused downtown via Marion Road where the handbags were tossed out of the vehicle. This scenario put Julian Berti particularly near to the action and if it was even close to the truth, it could be one reason why Berti did not choose to tell police everything that occurred that night. After all, it had been Julian Berti's brother who asked him to 'look after Frank' while he was in Adelaide. Julian Berti might have been worried he could be accused of being an accessory after the fact or he might have been worried the group involvement with the accused was because of his family's involvement with him. Either way Rofe proposed that Berti's evidence was important to assessing Scott Schinella.

The jury received a challenge from the Prosecutor. The seriousness of the charge was obvious. The inconsistencies and imperfections of the evidence of Schinella and Thallas were obvious. The fact the witnesses held onto this information for over two years was obvious. Why would they do that? Was it misguided loyalty to the group, fear of being involved, or fear of police and the courts? Until confronted by the police their version of events was hidden and because Schinella first lied to the police until his attack of conscience, his credibility became suspect. Thallas couldn't keep his story straight either, making his version equally suspect.

Had the Prosecutor given enough reasons for why these witnesses hid what they knew? Obviously if they had come forward within days of the murder there would have been no cause to question them in terms of credibility other than investigating their allegations. It would have made the police investigation so much easier if they had received this information closer to the murder.

From the perspective of the prosecution several questions arose from the evidence. The supposed concocted story between Thallas and Schinella was, to say the least, extraordinary. Why would Schinella put himself in the apartment within an hour of the killing? Why involve another person who could and did contradict his story? Why would there not be more detail given?

There is a very simple answer in my submission ladies and gentleman, that is, that finally the truth had been told. Much much to late, but it's finally come out, not because Thallas told him [Schinella] to [cover up for him] but because Schinella's conscience dictated it. He had lived with that knowledge for more than two years. And, as I said, the fact that he describes the words used by the accused in very similar terms doesn't echo concoction, but rather confirmation of what the accused said and what, indeed, and , in fact, happened. The police haven't found this unknown intervenor, said to have been stabbed by the accused. Wasn't that detail added by the accused as justification for his own actions? Trying to suggest to Schinella and Thallas, that this was a consensual sexual episode that got out of hand because some idiot who came round and hit him or kicked him or something 'and the girl strated screaming and I lost it and had to stab her.' When, really, we're talking about a sexual assault on a very drunken girl, clearly trying to defend herself. The cut skirt and so on.

The jury was reminded that they were dealing with ordinary people in an extraordinary situation and the system would be relying on their collective commonsense to discern whether they were telling the truth or not. To bring a conviction the jury had to be certain beyond any reasonable doubt that the accused told Schinella and Thallas, his mates at the time, what happened in the early hours of 6 June1993.

The Prosecutor asked the jury to look at all of the evidence, give it due regard and make allowances for obvious criticisms. Would Schinella, Thallas or Schilling concoct a story for $800? 'If you are satisfied that they are truthful about the critical conversation, whatever else you may think about their evidence, your duty is to return a verdict of guilty.' Paul Rofe returned to his seat behind the prosecution table. He had done his best.

Justice Mullighan invited Defence Counsel to deliver closing arguments on behalf of the accused. Counsel stood, walked deliberately toward the jury, making eye contact with as many as she could. The court waited in hushed anticipation. It was time to cement her case.

From the beginning Counsel purposefully attempted to tear down every shred of the Prosecutor's argument. She agreed with points not in dispute. She did not agree there were only three people who on oath said they did not kill Shirree.

What he [Rofe] missed out was the most important person in this trial who said, on oath, that he didn't kill Shirree Turner, and that, of course ladies and gentleman, is the accused.

Counsel reminded the jury the accused did not have to take the witness stand, be sworn, give evidence or be subjected to a long cross-examination.

Don't you think, ladies and gentleman, that the killer just got rid of those handbags as soon as he could after he left Oaklands Reserve in the panic that he must have been feeling at that particular time. Don't you think if that was anywhere near where you lived, he would have waited until he was right away from the scene, right away from where any connection could be made between him and the handbags before they would be dumped?

Counsel pointed out that the knife in evidence was not the murder weapon and was only a replica of the knife Thallas said he gave to the accused. Mercuri had not denied Thallas gave him a knife. He did however dispute the birthday gift was the same as the knife in evidence. The accused stated he received a double-edged knife which clipped onto a belt, and the Prosecutor had pointed out the importance of which knife was the birthday gift. 'Why shouldn't it be important? Wouldn't it be important to you in Mr Mercuri's position?' Defence claimed that the accused was not protesting too much or making too much of a point about the fact that the knife was double-bladed, and asserted that it couldn't have been the knife used in this murder.

According to Counsel, Thallas's evidence about the knives he purchased was inconsistent. For a start, Thallas had said he didn't remember he purchased two knives on the same day until faced with receipts. Secondly, he was certain the birthday gift was the same as the knife in evidence yet conceded in cross-examination it was possible it could have been the other knife. Thirdly, he was confused about the cost of the knives. Even though Ponting said he was certain the knife purchased as the birthday gift was the same as the single-bladed knife in evidence, Thallas conceded it was possible he had given the other knife, the double-bladed knife, to the accused.

Counsel suggested Ponting could have been mistaken about which knife was intended as the birthday gift. It was possible, in the opinion of Counsel, that the time frame between the purchase of the knives and giving his evidence in the trial confused his thinking. It was also possible that even if Thallas had in mind to give the single-bladed knife as the gift he could have had a change of heart.

Thallas's evidence was at odds with the accused on other aspects. Thallas said the accused told him he 'wouldn't mind owning a knife like that'. The accused denied he said anything of the kind. Thallas stated the accused was invited to have a look at what was sold in the back of the van. Ponting stated Thallas was by himself when the purchases were made. The single-bladed knife was put onto Thallas's account whereas the double-bladed knife was paid for with cash.

Counsel pointed out that a birthday gift was not a tax deduction and therefore suggested the cash receipt knife (the double-bladed knife) was more likely to be the one intended as a gift.

At this point it occurred to me that Thallas would not have purchased a gift in the presence of the recipient especially if it was intended to be a surprise. It was entirely possible Mercuri was inside the van checking out items for sale some time prior to the purchase, in which case he could have said he 'wouldn't mind owning a knife like that', giving Thallas a hint of what to buy his friend for his birthday. Why would Thallas want Mercuri to know he was giving him a knife for his birthday?

It was important to the Defence that many thousands of knives could fit the profile of the knife used in the murder. The fact the replica knife had a blade length of only nine centimetres and one of the wounds had a depth of sixteen centimetres added more to the equation.

Dr Gilbert formed an opinion the blade length was in all probability around fifteen centimetres before being presented with the replica knife. The addition of chest compression to the equation was only given to indicate that it was possible for a knife with a shorter blade length to be the culprit if used with sufficient force to deeply compress the chest.

Counsel continued to tear apart the evidence. Beginning with police interviews, the jury was reminded that Thallas told police the accused confessed to a murder. On the same day Schinella told police he knew nothing about any of the group doing harm to a woman and nobody ever asked him not to say anything.

Every piece of evidence was dissected and comparisons made. The evidence was linked with the saturation of publicity. Inference was made that Thallas's evidence about the woman in Rosina Street could have been taken from the newspaper and television publicity. A large number of calls resulted in a number of people being investigated about false stories motivated by malice or mischief. Counsel presented other reasons why people would lie. Her theory was that the evidence of Schinella and Thallas was no more credible than other false stories presented.

Counsel challenged the jury members to test the evidence of Thallas and Schinella carefully. Thallas and the accused continued their friendship until the utility incident early in 1994. They did not end the friendship immediately after the alleged confession of a shocking and horrific murder. 'Do you really think a man who has heard a confession to murder is going to go along with doing boy's stuff with the murderer?' In fact, Thallas was not sufficiently horrified enough, as a person might be in these circumstances, to not want to have anything to do with Mercuri. On the contrary, Thallas continued the friendship until early in 1994.

Defence Counsel conceded there was no evidence Thallas had been spreading malicious gossip but pointed out that the organised swoop by police on the group was conducted as a result of what police heard. It was also pointed out that in his first statement Thallas told police he did not know what they were talking about when confronted. Thallas must have been very worried about what the police knew. They had to know something to point them in his direction.

> *Don't you think, ladies and gentleman, that it is a very real possibility that Thallas, for whatever reason, whether he hates Mercuri, whether he is a big noter, whether there is some other motive we don't know about, that he [Thallas] has been saying these mailicious things. The police haul him in, he has to stick to his lie, he bolsters it by these falsehoods concerning Jacquie, he gets implicated and then he calls in his good mate, Scott Schinella, to get him out of it.*

He first denied the group spoke about this significant event, finally admitting under oath they briefly discussed the topic. To the defence it was ridiculous to think anyone could believe that this group, after a significant number of them were interviewed, would not have discussed the precarious situation they were now in, and at great length. After all, it was a bad situation. Thallas had stated that the group had sat down only for a brief minute and just talked about it quickly. To the Defence it seemed highly unlikely that the most important thing to happen to the group in their lifetime had been talked over in a brief minute, especially when Schinella would not even admit to a brief discussion.

Why were they refusing to acknowledge they must have discussed such a significant event in detail? It was suggested the answer lay in the probable story concocted between Schinella and Thallas. Counsel compared their scenario with other versions of events and went on to state why theirs proved to be false and misleading. The only difference between other false stories and this scenario was that the other lies did not lead to a man being charged with the most serious charge of murder. The most telling piece of evidence about Thallas and Schilling seeing the accused with a woman in Rosina Street was that she was speaking another language.

> *Don't you think, ladies and gentlemen of the jury, that if she could speak another language, the prosecution would have called evidence to establish the young woman speaking a foreign language was in fact Shirree Turner?*

It was the submission of Defence Counsel that the woman spoken of by Thallas and his girlfriend was a different woman, and quite possibly on a different night. It was also Defence's submission that the night the accused came home in a bad mood and found Schinella and Julian Berti in his apartment was another night.

Having explored the inconsistencies of the evidence from Thallas, Counsel shifted her focus to Schinella. Schinella's confession about his hurried exit from the apartment was also full of holes. 'How can he be hearing a confession of murder at 2 am on the morning of Sunday 6 June 1993, when Ms Turner's not dead at 2 am?' In the opinion of the Defence, Schinella's proposed time frame of events and the estimated time of Shirree's death, did not match up.

There were fundamental flaws in Schinella's version. His evidence about what he did before arriving at the apartment was never questioned. There was no contradiction by any of the people who Schinella was with prior to arriving at the apartment about what time he left them. He left his girlfriend immediately prior to passing by the apartment and Schinella's girlfriend did not contradict his timing in her statement.

Counsel was not convinced, even with the passage of time between the alleged confession and Schinella's interview over two years later, that it warranted consideration he might have been mistaken about the times.

The court adjourned for a lunch break. My head was spinning. I was trying very hard to keep thinking positive thoughts but the look on the faces of friends and family told me I was wasting my time. Counsel had succeeded in creating so much doubt it would have taken a brave jury to convict on the basis of what they had heard so far.

Although convinced of Mercuri's guilt, I could see that the Prosecutor had been pushing against the tide. The decision to prosecute was correct but we didn't have the credible witnesses or admissible evidence to strengthen our case and my fear of the worst scenario happening was increasing markedly.

With the luncheon adjournment over, Defence Counsel continued her closing argument. Schinella's evidence did not make sense in relation to timing and it was unlikely fear was a factor. Schinella obviously did not think his story through or he would have realised the accused would not have confessed to murder several hours before he committed it. He had obviously not thought much about making his story believable. Was he that stupid?

Counsel compared the man seen with Shirree with descriptions given by witnesses who knew the accused in 1993. The man seen with Shirree was described as having short hair in front and longish hair at the back, in line with the fashion at the time. Witnesses, who knew the accused, stated that he had shorter hair than was the fashion at the back and was receding in front. Were they telling the truth or were they covering?

Defence Counsel cleverly linked the available evidence and compared it to what Schinella and Thallas had testified. Their glaring inconsistencies were made more than obvious. The ingenuity of Counsel was fascinating to watch. The difference in the length of hair and the description of the clothes the accused wore, compared with what Cherry saw and testified to, suggested two different men. It was strange how Schinella and his friends could remember what Mercuri wore or how he wore his hair yet they had great difficulty recalling the important details.

Counsel raised the issue of the police folders containing photos of similar-looking men. The jury couldn't view them because the folders were dismantled and even though they were re-assembled in 1997 the folders were not exactly the same. It was a highly unsatisfactory situation, according to Counsel, who thought police were remiss in handling some of the evidence especially in regard to the photos and the knives. The police were portrayed as inept and Counsel continued in her attempt to discredit them at every opportunity.

Returning to the evidence given by Schinella and Thallas, Counsel systematically discounted every detail piece by piece. She dismissed as 'nonsense' the alleged story about another man being stabbed in the same incident. There was no police or hospital report of a stabbing to substantiate that story. 'It's a matter for you to assess the witness and you might have thought that Mr Schinella wasn't the brightest man you've ever seen', and he's 'simply incapable of telling a consistent story', Counsel argued. He and Thallas told such a web of lies they found they couldn't extricate themselves and so 'he vacillates between fear—fear of what we ask—and this notion of confusion, slip of the tongue, mixed up words, got confused'.

With the vital evidence of Julian Berti totally contradicting Schinella's version the prosecution's case was crumbling. Berti had stated he 'heard nothing about any confession and didn't remember the accused coming home with dirt on his clothes and face'. Counsel accused Schinella of lying to protect Thallas who, in their view, put him up to telling a story.

The evidence of the accused was the last issue covered by Counsel. Mercuri was described as a man with no family in the State or any other reference points for remembering specific dates except perhaps birthdays. According to Counsel that made it understandable if he had trouble recalling certain dates and times and was even more understandable given that he was confronted with an accusation of murder more than two years after it occurred.

If, at the end of the day you don't know what to believe, you don't know whether to believe Schinella or whether to believe Berti, then you must acquite Mr Mercuri. You don't have to say I believe one or I believe the other. It's our submission of course, that you will disbelieve Schinella but it might be, at the end of the day, that you won't know who to believe and so, in our submission, that will lead you to the acquittal of Mr Mercuri based on this so called confession to Schinella.

Justice Mullighan prepared to deliver his summing up. I was very relieved the trial had reached this point but I was worried about the result. I did not want to lose hope, it was about all I had to hang on to, but it was entirely possible that within the next twenty-four hours we would have a verdict. It was impossible to predict how long the Judge would take and it was equally impossible to predict how long it would take the jury to deliberate on their decision. It was very likely that a decision would not be made before the end of the following day.

Justice Mullighan began his address to a hushed court. Everybody present, especially the press, wanted to hear every word. I looked slowly around the court. Every eye was focused intently on the judge.

Ladies and gentlemen, we have now reached the stage of the trial where it is my duty to sum up the case to you ... In summing up I will have something to say about the law, and I also shall have something to say about the facts ... In discharging your function in this case you will bear in mind the importance of a criminal trial, from the point of view of the accused, and also the community. It is obviously important, to say the least, for the accused. He has been charged with a serious crime and he is

not to be convicted on insufficient or doubtful evidence. It is also impor-
tant to the community, for the criminal courts exist for the protection of
the public, and if the charge has been proven beyond reasonable doubt,
then it is your duty to say so.

Justice Mullighan described the witnesses as people of different back-
grounds, ages, experiences, occupations, levels of general knowledge and
intelligence. The evidence of all of the witnesses was crucial and the
jury's assessment of the witnesses should be approached with a view to
the importance of such evidence to the entire case. He explained that it
was for them to decide whether they believed all or part of the evidence
of a witness.

The accused is entitled to have his evidence assessed, scrutinised and eval-
uated in the same way as any other witness in the case, and you must
bring a fair and impartial judgement to bear upon the evidence. It would
be quite wrong to disregard the evidence of the accused. Obviously he has
an interest in exonerating himself.

Emphasis was placed on the elapsed time between the murder and
the trial.

The delay should not be used as an explanation or a substitute for reliable
and convincing evidence. You must assess all of the evidence without emo-
tion ... Clearly, this case involves a very real personal tragedy. A young
woman has lost her life. She met her death violently. She was viciously
attacked with a knife and brutally stabbed many times in a deserted park.
She was left to die. She struggled her way some 80 metres or so to try and
obtain help, and died at the front door of a stranger. A night of celebration,
which began in such high spirits, ended you may well conclude, in a brutal
murder. That, in itself, is very likely to evoke strong emotions. It is not dif-
ficult to feel outrage and indignation at what was done to Ms Turner.

Justice Mullighan discussed the many pieces of evidence that might produce feelings of sympathy, prejudice or other emotional responses. 'Although these feelings are very natural, you must exclude them from your consideration of the evidence.'

The jury was directed to apply their collective commonsense to free and frank discussion of the evidence. Different categories of evidence were raised and explanations of the law as it related to the case given. It was late in the afternoon when Justice Mullighan adjourned the proceedings. He rose and left the bench.

The final day of the trial began. Justice Mullighan finished his address. The issue for the jury to decide was whether the accused was the attacker. The Judge went on to specify the unusual features of the case. There were no eyewitnesses to the murder. There was no evidence given to show how Shirree came to be at Oaklands Reserve. The murder weapon was never found. There was no evidence that with any certainty linked the accused to the scene of the murder. There was no DNA evidence or transference of fragments or particles from the accused to Shirree. The sexual assault did not constitute rape because no semen was found that could have identified her attacker. The police investigation was extensive but did not lead to an arrest in 1993. There was a substantial delay before any criminal action was taken.

> *Unless you are satisfied about the evidence of one of them, you must find the accused not guilty … [Another possibility for you to consider] is that, after full and careful consideration, of all of the evidence, you are unable to say where the truth lies and you are unable to say who is telling the truth … you will find the accused not guilty.*

Justice Mullighan, after final instructions, completed his summation of the evidence. The jury retired with the responsibility of sorting through all of the evidence. I did not envy them. It was going to be an awesome task if they had not already made up their minds.

Justice Mullighan told both attorneys he would not take a verdict before 2 pm. How could they possibly come to such an important decision in one hour? Had the Judge and both defence and prosecution counsels already decided what the decision was going to be? Had the jury members reached the same conclusion? Justice Mullighan left the bench a little after 1 pm.

'Why don't you all go somewhere and have a coffee?' The sheriff's officer suggested. 'It could be some time before they come back. It'll be at least an hour and I'll contact you if you need to come back.' My friends and I went to a café close by.

Defence Counsel looked reasonably confident. She had cause to be feeling pleased with her efforts. The prosecution team was at best hopeful that the jury would be able to see through the lies, deceit and downright stupidity of some of the witnesses and come to the right conclusion.

I knew my family and friends were all hoping for the right decision but I also knew Defence Counsel had presented a brilliant argument and, even though the flaws in Mercuri's testimony were obvious to me, the jury had to assess the evidence according to law and the evidence presented. They didn't have access to the information I had about the character of the man accused of murdering my daughter. The jury did not know that Mercuri was being transported to court each day from jail or that he was serving a sentence for a similar crime.

To the jury, Mercuri appeared innocent. How much doubt had been raised? All they saw was a young man who sat quietly in the dock looking the picture of innocence. His testimony was naturally going to be in direct contrast to the witnesses who testified against him. I could only hope that if the Defence could create doubt about the truthfulness of Schinella and Thallas then it was reasonable to believe Frank Mercuri might also be lying.

Nine women and three men now had the unenviable task of reaching a verdict. I could only hope they would be guided by commonsense even if they did not have all of the information about Mercuri's character. My chief worry all along had been that the jury could not possibly make a fair judgment without knowing something about Mercuri's character and past criminal history.

I wanted to prepare my family and friends for the possibility of a 'not guilty' verdict, but how could I dash their hopes? I was desperately trying to remain positive even though the sense of foreboding I had felt in the police car on the way to the morgue was back with me again.

I tried to go over the past two weeks in my head. Even though I had not been inside the courtroom when the majority of evidence was presented, my family, friends and the media journalists who covered the trial informed me of the events each day. I had a good idea of what had transpired and was about as confident as the Prosecutor about the outcome.

There were still times when I thought, this has to be some kind of dream. Surely, this is not real? It's just not happening. But reality bit into my thoughts and although acceptance was difficult it was always inevitable. How many times in the past five years had I found myself in the same situation, trying to shake myself back to reality?

The jury, in all probability, would not take too long to reach a verdict. The entire future of another human being was in their hands. It had to be an awesome responsibility. I could only hope they realised that my future and that of my family and Shirree's friends was also hanging in the balance. I prayed silently, as I had done so many times in the past five years, that God would bring a sense of discernment into their thinking and their discussions.

I knew the evidence presented leaned heavily in favour of the accused. I could only hope the jury would be able to see though the lies, but reality told me it would be difficult to convict on what this jury had to go on.

A few minutes before 3 pm we were asked to return to the courtroom. The jury had reached a verdict after only two hours of deliberations.

It had been nearly five years since Shirree's death and it had all come down to the next few moments. Justice Mullighan returned to the bench and the jury, with sombre faces, filed into the jury box to take their seats for the final time.

Chapter 13

The Verdict

The only sounds I could hear were quiet whispers and shuffling feet. It seemed the entire courtroom was holding its breath in anticipation. An eerie silence prevailed for a few moments as tension continued to build. I was tense, all my thoughts focused on willing the jury to find in favour of the prosecution. The Clerk called the court to order and Justice Mullighan addressed the jury. 'Ladies and gentlemen of the jury,' the Judge stated officially, 'have you reached a verdict in the case of the Crown versus Frank Mercuri?' The tension was almost unbearable.

'We have, Your Honour,' came the sombre reply.

The Clerk, who had been handed the verdict details, placed the vital piece of paper before the Judge who scanned it quickly before speaking. 'How say you? Do you find the accused in this case guilty or not guilty?'

The young man elected as spokesperson said soberly, 'We, the jury in this case, find the accused not guilty.' It was unanimous. All twelve jurors had voted to acquit the accused.

The chaotic scenes following the verdict could only be described as pandemonium. Print journalists rushed out of court to phone their editors. Court reporters from the television stations left to join their camera teams outside to prepare for filming interviews. The news services would have a field day with this verdict.

Paul Rofe tore the wig from his head and threw it angrily onto the table. He had known going in the case was weak. The time frame between the murder and the trial was too long to depend on memories being reliable. He had done his very best with what he was able to present in court. He'd relied on witnesses whose only consistency was the frequency of their changing stories. He'd had to put up with witnesses who lied to cover up their own inadequacies and ultimately these conditions made his task untenable.

His disappointment was obvious and I felt real sympathy for him, even in my own disappointment. I could feel the frustration of the whole prosecution team. They knew as well as I did what the accused was all about and he had just been acquitted of murder. The admissible evidence may not have been enough to convict him in the eyes of the law but that did not mean that he was innocent in the eyes of the Prosecutor, the police or my supporters and me.

I was standing with the Prosecutor and didn't notice Defence Counsel approach with an outstretched hand. 'No hard feelings,' she said and I shook her hand automatically. Feelings? What feelings? I was numb. I didn't have any feelings. I looked slowly around the court and could see the police investigators who had worked so hard on the case shaking their heads with dismay. They had watched the entire case collapse before their eyes. They believed a travesty of justice had just taken place.

Once again, forgetting my own pain, I could feel their frustration. All the work they had done on this case must have seemed to be in vain. The case had collapsed like a house of cards. Nearly five years of preparation by the police and the prosecutor's office for this moment and the jury had taken not much more than an hour to reach a decision.

I searched the court for family, knowing the devastation they must be feeling. I caught sight of them almost running outside. I wanted to talk with them and offer comfort but it was too late to stop them. They would be trying to avoid cameras and journalists. I could understand my family's grief as they hoped for a different ending. What they could not possibly see was the epic proportions the jury's decision was going to take on in the coming months. Not even I could foresee what the future held. At that moment I could see very little future at all.

After spending some time discussing the outcome of the case with the Prosecutor and the detectives I realised I was not able to take in much of what they were saying and it was time to face the press. 'Obviously I'm disappointed but I do believe the prosecution did all it could possibly do,' I stated simply in response to the questions as I left the building.

I was determined not to lose it now. I'd been able to keep it all together so far and for my family's sake I wanted to remain strong. I had hoped I might be able to go home and begin to put the nightmare behind me but that was not possible now. Hope for an end to the traumas I'd been through was dashed by two words—not guilty.

I had just finished talking to reporters when I became aware of a disturbance not far away. Turning toward the noise I saw Fabio leaving the building. Angry that his mother had been humiliated by Defence Counsel and by the Judge's summing-up speech, and very disappointed about the verdict, he kicked out at the cameras. His reaction to the reporter's question would make sensational news that evening.

I felt sorry for Fabio and knowing he was not noted for being calm under pressure, I moved to try to restrain him. A detective standing nearby helped force Fabio back inside the building. We tried to convince him that it would do no good to behave in that manner. He wasn't listening.

'Fab, you have to keep your temper under control. It's enough that your little display will probably be splashed over television screens tonight. You're only going to make an idiot out of yourself if you carry on this way.'

'Listen to Ken,' the detective said. 'It's good advice.'

Fabio glared at both of us. He was breathing heavily and his fiery eyes darted between us. 'I understand your frustration and your anger, Fab, but you have to get a grip on yourself. Calm down. Think about it. Look, I know it's hard but you can't do anything about it now. And you'll just make a fool out of yourself if you throw tantrums.'

Finally, Fabio calmed down enough to leave the building peaceably. I breathed a sigh of relief. I didn't need to be dealing with that type of behaviour even though I understood why Fabio reacted. I just wanted to get away somewhere and think quietly. I was accepting what happened in the sense I could do nothing to reverse the jury's decision. I was physically and emotionally exhausted but I felt a strange sense of calm as well. At the same time I knew it was not over, not by a long shot.

I wasn't going to leave it behind and just get on with my life. I was not the type of person who could drop an issue that weighed heavily on me. I felt I would be letting Shirree down if I just crawled into a corner now and licked my wounds. I was determined her murder would not be swept under any carpet.

It might be impossible to obtain justice through the criminal justice system but I was bound by a parental sense of responsibility. I was not going to be able to leave it alone until completely satisfied I'd done all I could for Shirree. 'If there is a way, Shirree, I'll find it. I can promise you that.'

I could not put Shirree's murder to rest. I felt a travesty of justice had occurred and I was not satisfied there was no other avenue I could pursue. Newspaper and television items in the days following the trial kept the issue of the murder and the acquittal alive for a short time. Fiona Clark wrote about the acquittal in *The Advertiser* under the headline, 'So who killed Shirree?'[7]

'Frank Mercuri closed his eyes and breathed a sigh of relief before hanging his head in his hands and smiling,' Fiona wrote. The article briefly covered the murder and the trial.

Justice Mullighan was reported to have congratulated the jury on their decision after thanking them for their time and consideration. 'If I may say so, given the state of the evidence in all the matters you have heard, your verdict is an entirely proper one,' the Judge said.

I was extremely disappointed the Judge made such an unfeeling statement. I felt it was both unnecessary and terribly insensitive toward my family and Shirree's friends. I understood the Judge would want to thank the jury for their diligence but to state their decision was 'an entirely proper one' hurt me deeply and several people in contact with me from the media agreed the remark was unwarranted.

Still in shock about the acquittal I read another article written the Saturday following the trial. Fiona Clark's exposé about Mercuri's past criminal history covered the truth about the accused, which I felt the jury should have been told.

Under the headline 'Exposed: the dark side of Frank Mercuri',[8] Fiona wrote that Mercuri was back in jail in Victoria to serve out the remainder of a sentence for the stabbing and attempted rape of a woman on New Year's Eve 1994. It was reported Mercuri had hardly seen the outside of a prison since the age of nineteen and was now twenty-six. He'd been sentenced in 1995 by a Melbourne court to four years with a minimum term of thirty-three months for attempted rape and intentionally causing serious injury.

The article reported details of the crime. Mercuri was, up until the 1995 trial in Victoria, predominantly a petty criminal. He'd been convicted forty-eight times and appeared in court ten times. Convictions included attempted armed robbery, recklessly causing injury, dishonesty and car theft.

I obtained a copy of the sentencing report from Mercuri's previous court case. The maximum penalty could have totalled twenty-seven years and six months. Mercuri received four years with a non-parole period of thirty-three months, even after an extensive life of previous criminal behaviour.

Kellam, the judge in Mercuri's previous trial, described the attack on the woman in graphic detail, calling the attack 'horrific and extremely violent' and stated it was an abuse of the woman's friendship. Her victim impact statement described the episode as 'one of great horror and fear'. She referred to her 'disappointment at the breach of her trust in him as a friend'.

Judge Kellam had said in his 1995 sentencing report that Mercuri had led a life of deprivation and hardship. He'd been abandoned by his mother to the care of an abusive father and was placed in care at the age of thirteen. He then stayed with grandparents for three years. This was the only period of stability in his life. Then for a short time he lived with his mother again. Mercuri lost his job as a boilermaker and ended up sleeping in parks. His criminal life started when he stole cars to sleep in on rainy nights.

Did this life of apparent deprivation give him the right to turn to a life of crime? I wondered why the courts continued to give chance after chance to this man who, by his own record, hadn't learned much about turning his life around. Jail terms had done nothing to assist him to realise that a life of crime was unacceptable.

Mercuri had denied attempting to rape the woman but said she'd been stabbed in the course of a scuffle. He'd shown so much concern after the stabbing that he'd pushed her over the first floor balcony into a car park below. I was astounded that these 'instances' were not considered as attempted murder.

Mercuri's grandparents attended court and a reference by an employer kept alive his prospect for rehabilitation. A psychological evaluation showed no significant psychiatric or psychological factor existed to give any excuse for his behaviour. Mercuri's counsel appealed for leniency in sentencing, citing the hardship and deprivation of his background.

Judge Kellam decided that despite the seriousness of the offences, Mercuri might still rehabilitate himself and lead a decent life. His decision to sentence Mercuri to four years out of a possible twenty-seven and a half was typical of the leniency in sentencing that was taking place all over the country.

Forty-eight previous convictions for past offences spoke volumes about his attempt to rehabilitate himself. At least part of every year for the previous five years had been spent in prison for various offences, including violent crimes. This time his propensity for violence was taken out on a woman who called him a friend. She could have lost her life. What more did this man need to do to prove he was a menace to society?

My sense of outrage for the woman ran very deep. What went through her mind when Mercuri was given such a manifestly inadequate sentence? I could only imagine how cheated she must have felt until the same disappointment in the justice system happened to me. Now I had a good idea how the system can treat a victim. Victims are given a mandatory life sentence. This woman would never forget what 'her friend' did to her and the situation was made worse by the justice system. Where was her justice?

Chapter 14

Pursuing Justice

A week after the end of the criminal trial I consented to an interview with *The Advertiser*. The morning newspaper carried the headline, 'The daughter I'll never forget'.[9] Since Shirree's death I had compiled a folder full of memories of tragedy, disappointment and yet I still had hope. I'd made a decision to try to turn the tragedy into something more positive. Any reminder of the daughter I missed so much was placed into the folder. The memories were building into a picture that would gently and beautifully remind me of how incredibly sweet every shared moment was. Details faded with the passing of time but I had photographs, notes, cards, letters and video footage of her twenty-first birthday, diaries and other memorabilia to refresh my memory.

I used my time with the youth group to do some research. I posed questions to teenagers and people in their early twenties to find out what they thought about certain scenarios. The feedback I received only served to increase my alarm.

It seemed to me that many young people were blissfully unaware of the dangerous situations they could get themselves into simply by ignoring personal safety measures. They seemed to think that just because they were young nothing bad could happen to them.

I discussed my thoughts on the subject with Fiona and she included some hard-hitting realities in her article. She wrote about how I begged Shirree not to frequent the clubs she liked to go to and the devastation I felt when the police asked me to identify my daughter's body. I talked about my relationship with Shirree and how precious it was. 'She was my best friend, my buddy and my mate. We built up a relationship that was going to last the rest of our lives. I didn't realise she would die before me,' I told Fiona sadly. Shirree did not normally drink heavily but I admitted on that fateful night she 'drank far too much'.

The questions left unanswered by the acquittal were a further devastating blow for family and friends. My desire to tell young people in particular about her story renewed my interest in having a book written which I hoped would deal principally with the investigation by the police and the trial. It would be the untold story.

This and other projects in the pipeline were all designed to ensure that Shirree's death was not forgotten, all the more important to me because of another recent spate of murders. I wanted to encourage the community to create vibrant and safe places for young people to go on Friday and Saturday nights to replace the Hindley Street nightclub strip.

Several journalists were interested in keeping in touch. I had the feeling they were quite cynical about the justice system and my story was fodder for their journalistic expertise. The fact that I was always prepared to talk gave them an avenue to pursue when they needed my point of view for an article

A few days after the acquittal one of my new journalist friends made an astounding suggestion, 'Why don't you do an OJ Simpson on this guy?'

What did it mean? I remembered the OJ Simpson case very well. OJ Simpson had been acquitted by a United States criminal court for murder. However, a civil court had then ruled that OJ Simpson was responsible for the deaths of Nicole Simpson and Ron Goldman and awarded the plaintiffs millions of dollars in damages. OJ has never paid out any of the damages, citing that the cost of defending himself in court had left him with no money. I suspected that the primary motivation of the plaintiffs in launching the action had not been for the money but to ensure that the person responsible for the two deaths was brought to justice. But this had all taken place in the United States where actions of this kind were not an unusual occurrence.

Still, the idea persisted and I began to wonder if it could be done in an Australian civil court. I continued to mull over the idea of instigating proceedings. I had a lot to consider. Would my health stand up to the strain of another court battle? I was still visiting several doctors who were monitoring me closely.

Also, what would it cost? Civil actions could be expensive and I didn't have the means to take on massive legal costs. Since I could not make a firm decision I decided to seek legal advice and contacted a lawyer. John Doherty, or JD as he was widely known, was an experienced and well-respected litigation lawyer. He was interested in the case from the beginning. JD knew about the criminal case, its high profile and was aware the public was not happy with the outcome of the trial. There had been considerable outrage about the verdict, particularly in light of the facts revealed in the newspaper a few days after the acquittal. It was rumoured that many law firms were dissatisfied with the handling of some cases in the criminal courts.

I discussed at length with JD the feasibility of instigating a civil action against Mercuri for wrongful death. JD was very eager to accept the challenge. I breathed a sigh of relief when told it was possible even though proceedings of this type had never been attempted in Australia. JD's enthusiasm was infectious.

Since the action was going to be a first in Australia, careful attention needed to be paid to keep the public informed. The legal profession and the justice system as a whole would be watching the case carefully, scrutinising every detail closely.

Peter Campbell, an entertainment lawyer and expert in negotiating contracts, was engaged to handle the publicity and contracts with the media. Peter immediately approached Channel Nine's national current affairs program, *A Current Affair*, who were keen to obtain exclusive rights to the story. Included in the deal was at least one article in the national weekly women's magazine *Woman's Day*.

While JD was hard at work on the case I employed an assistant. Lesley, who was willing to type letters for me and helped with research into the Similar Fact Evidence law. It was an issue that had taken on huge proportions in my mind. No-one seemed to be able to explain why Similar Fact Evidence could not have been used in the criminal trial. The case in which Mercuri stabbed another young woman while attempting to rape her held similar enough issues to what had occurred before Shirree was murdered.

For some time I had been concerned that certain material was not admissible evidence in a criminal trial. I understood the theory behind past criminal history being inadmissible, although I disagreed with it. I firmly believed if certain evidence had been allowed into court, the outcome of the trial would have been very different. I felt the votes of the jury would have been different had the truth about Mercuri's past been told in court. I wondered how many others might have felt the same and decided differently if they had known.

The most glaring question was, how can a jury make a fair decision when they don't have all the facts? It was particularly pertinent when faced with 'similar facts' about a person's character and criminal history. Mercuri's propensity to violent behaviour, especially toward women, was known. His criminal record was testament to that fact. The word 'similar' indicated that the facts did not have to be exactly the same. So the conviction Mercuri had on his record for attempted rape and assault causing actual bodily injury seemed to qualify in similarity.

Shirree died from the stab wounds while the other young woman survived, but not for his lack of trying to kill her. After several stab wounds in a frenzied attack, escaping, then being captured again by Mercuri and pushed over a balcony, it seemed to me there was enough intent to kill her. The woman involved had told police that Mercuri said he 'had to kill her'. On the surface it seemed she was very fortunate to have survived.

The more I delved into Similar Fact Evidence the more confused I became about its application in a case. It didn't make much sense to me but it was becoming apparent that the use of this particular law was generally avoided. It seemed so complex that its complexity might be the reason it was rarely used.

I wrote letters to politicians, the judge, and the premier of South Australia in an attempt to find answers to the many questions I had surrounding the acquittal. I wanted to know the exact reasons why Similar Fact Evidence could not have been used. I couldn't get a clear answer from anyone as to why this could not be used in Mercuri's trial. It was understandable that defence attorneys would not be happy about its use in a trial as it would be a disadvantage to their clients, but I still came back to my original question. How can a jury make a fair verdict without all the known facts?

Several weeks passed. Late one afternoon I received a phone call that completely threw me. The senior partners of the firm where JD worked had dropped a bombshell during a board meeting, asking him to withdraw from the case. They held the view that since they always fought for justice in the traditional way, they were not prepared to allow JD to take on such a controversial case. My case was therefore unacceptable to them and JD was ordered to immediately withdraw his services. He was furious but had to bow to their wishes, however reluctantly. He could not talk them into changing their mind.

When JD informed me of the partners' decision I was stunned. It was another slap in the face. Was there any justice to be found anywhere? I was already a victim of a travesty of justice from the criminal system, now it seemed that the pursuit of justice was to be denied to me again. It always seemed that the odds were stacked against me.

I paced around for some time trying to figure out what to do next. I called Peter Campbell, who was handling the media negotiations. Peter told me the decision by the law firm was inappropriate. His advice was to put them on notice that an action would be initiated for additional costs incurred in re-negotiating the media contracts; the firm had placed the contracts in some jeopardy by their decision. After talking with Peter and receiving advice I felt better. I was still apprehensive but a little calmer. A civil action was expensive. I had been quoted enormous amounts and I didn't have anywhere near the kind of money being quoted. The Supreme Court trial was funded by the State but a civil action was my responsibility.

Undeterred, I pressed on. It was essential another law firm be found to handle the litigation as soon as possible. There had to be a firm in Adelaide courageous enough to take on this groundbreaking civil action. A journalist friend, Nick Colquhoun from Channel Nine, became the knight in shining armour. He suggested that I speak to Ron Bentley of Tindall, Gask & Bentley. His suggestion came at just the right time. Tindall, Gask & Bentley had a fine reputation in legal circles. I contacted Ron Bentley and discovered that there would be no hitches this time. After a short discussion, I was introduced to a highly recommended young lawyer. I found Charles Morland Bailes to be a personable young man. His calm, affable nature impressed me, but most importantly, he had a sound knowledge of the law.

Morry, as he was known, and his associate Brendan Connell willingly accepted the opportunity to represent me and immediately began work on what was to be a long and arduous preparation. The case was destined to make Australian legal history and they were both very happy to be a part of it. We could not afford any flaws or mistakes in our preparation. It was no small task, but the eyes of Australia would be watching us. Whatever the outcome of the action, the reputation of both lawyers and the firm they represented was going to be on the line.

I was determined to continue the campaign to search for answers to the many questions that were raised during the criminal trial. The questions had rattled around inside my head since the end of the criminal trial. Apart from the Similar Fact Evidence issue, I also wondered why the system seemed to lean toward the rights of the accused more than those of the victim. It seemed to me like an accused had it easy in court. They were innocent until proven guilty beyond a reasonable doubt. But what constituted reasonable doubt? I didn't think that it was fair that an accused does not have to do a thing to prove his innocence. They do not have to take the stand in their own defence. They do not have to say a thing.

Mercuri had decided to take the stand but at the end of the day all he did was refute what Thallas and Schinella said. In the end, it came down to his word against theirs. Schinella had proved he could tell lies and so had Thallas to a degree. But what about Mercuri? He had said in court that 'he didn't use knives'. That was a lie. He knew knives, or at least knew them well enough to have used one on his victim on New Year's Eve 1994, but the majority of the court knew nothing of this.

Two weeks after the criminal trial I was invited to see the Judge. I was curious about the reason and approached Justice Mullighan's chamber nervously. For ninety minutes we discussed many things about the case and about the legal system. The Judge was concerned for me about Shirree's murder and the effect the acquittal had on me. 'Had the trial been before a judge without a jury the same verdict would have been reached,' the Judge said. 'If a murder happened in my family I would find it very difficult to cope.'

I asked the Judge for the reasons why he considered Similar Fact Evidence law was not admissible in the criminal trial of the Crown vs Mercuri. 'From a victim's point of view I find it very unsatisfactory that crucial evidence was not allowed. As far as I am concerned it was the reason he [Mercuri] was acquitted. I'll never accept that he didn't kill her,' I told the Judge.

'Fortunately, in our free society, we can believe what we want,' the Judge said. 'I don't know what more I can say to help you understand what the law means in this case.' Justice Mullighan's explanation did not satisfy me. I still felt there was something inherently wrong with a system that allowed a murderer to go free due to a lack of admissible evidence when there was, in my opinion, ample evidence pointing to guilt.

'I know a lot of time has elapsed since the murder and there were a lot of obstacles for the Prosecutor to overcome, but the system favoured Mercuri a little too much for my liking. I can't believe the accused doesn't have to prove a thing. They can just sit in the dock, looking a picture of innocence. Okay, so Mercuri took the stand but exactly what did he say to convince anyone he didn't do it? Nothing he said enlightened the court about where he was on the night in question. He was clear about details pointing away from his guilt but no memory that would throw any light to his innocence. He used the presumption of innocence according to the law and that was all he needed.

'If, as I believe, Mercuri murdered Shirree, why would he admit to where he was on that weekend? He didn't have to, did he? He used presumption of innocence to his full advantage. Had he "remembered" exactly where he was and what he did and could prove it, he would have had a legitimate alibi and no charge could have been laid. But he couldn't do that, he couldn't remember. He did not give the authorities anything that could be checked out. Why? Because he didn't have to prove a thing.'

I nursed a theory that Mercuri's long criminal history gave him an edge. He knew what to say in court. He had a long time to think about what he could and couldn't admit to. If Schinella and Thallas were proven to have lied then wasn't it reasonable to believe Mercuri and Berti could have lied also? These and other questions continued burn inside me.

The jury's decision was also discussed with the Judge. In fairness to the jury they did not have all of the facts and with the doubt raised in the trial they could hardly have reached any other conclusion. But I did not have to accept the decision. Mercuri had his acquittal, but what did my family and friends have? They had endless unanswered questions and little satisfaction.

I left the Judge's chamber none the wiser. I was grateful for the interest in my predicament but still wondered what the purpose of the visit was. After thinking things through I was more settled about the decision to pursue justice through the less demanding Civil Court. If I could gain some justice for my daughter it would be the last gift I could give her.

I had several meetings with Morry and Brendan to discuss strategy. The Supreme Court demanded proof beyond any reasonable doubt but the Civil Court operated on the less demanding balance of probabilities. It meant we only had to prove Mercuri probably committed the crime and support it with enough evidence for a successful suit. This time there would be no secrets about Mercuri's past criminal history. Everything about his character, his propensity to violence, the similar offence committed against a 'friend' and other violent crimes would be out in the open.

John McAvoy, producer of *A Current Affair*, finally contacted me to arrange for Mike Munro and a team of camera and sound personnel to film the story. The magazine's Leonie Dale and a photographer finalised details to do the interview for *Woman's Day*. I was excited, but the pressure was still taking a toll.

The build-up toward the civil action was a busy time and I felt my life was about to turn a corner. I was still experiencing sleepless nights and nightmares when I did fall into an uneasy sleep but with the fullness of my days I seemed to cope. I was now able to share my burdens with people who understood where I was coming from and wanted to see that I took care of myself. My new assistant was a tower of strength, allowing me to unload some of the burdens I had carried around for so long. I found that releasing the pain I held by talking frankly about Shirree's death helped tremendously.

Since returning to Adelaide I had experienced more nightmares and panic attacks. The intensity of grief I felt after each nightmare seemed to increase dramatically. The content of the dreams had changed somewhat and this frightened me. I could not forget the scenes witnessed when I went to the place where Shirree died. Nor could I forget the trail of blood from the reserve, the painted outline on the porch where her body was found, or the two bloodied imprints of her hands on the wall just below the doorbell when she attempted to get help. The image of the blue bag containing Shirree's body being removed from the porch and placed into the coroner's ambulance, witnessed from television news broadcasts, played over and over in my mind.

I didn't know how to turn off my thoughts. My mind was so active with the pursuit of the civil action. I had to remember aspects of the time before Shirree's death through to the identification of her body to help with the legal proceedings. Painful issues had to be raised and faced again. With my mind still not able to let go of the images I couldn't imagine ever being able to forget. Would I ever live a normal life again?

My lawyers wanted me to be clear about what impact the images of Shirree's murder had on me as a victim. It was important, vital in fact, that I was able to verbalise my feelings and state of mind so the doctor's assessment of my psychological status would paint an accurate picture of how Shirree's death had impacted my life. I would be required to show how ongoing frustration brought on by the acquittal, unanswered questions and the terrible images conjured by Shirree's murder had contributed to my health problems.

The uncertainty of not knowing how Shirree ended up with her killer and why she went willingly with a complete stranger still bothered me. Accepting her death in conjunction with the outcome of the criminal trial was impossible without answers to my questions. It seemed there would be no respite from the emotional rollercoaster.

Dr Williams was very concerned. The lawyers contacted her and she knew her assessment would play an important part in the civil action. The court required documentation to prove nervous shock resulting in post-traumatic stress disorder (PTSD) in conjunction with other evidence supporting our claim that Mercuri was responsible for Shirree's murder. It was critical to my case that Dr Williams's assessment showed how firstly the murder and then the acquittal had produced nervous shock followed by the diagnosis of PTSD. The ongoing stress I was experiencing had to be documented accurately.

Dr Williams told me my feelings and reactions were normal. 'You've been through a terrible experience. You cannot be expected to feel any different. I know these are clichés but you need to know that whatever you are thinking and feeling is completely normal under these circumstances.'

She encouraged me not to internalise my feelings. 'Letting off steam, getting your anger out in the open, is a normal reaction to horrific circumstances. Don't you think that your family and friends would understand if you just blew up every now and then? Of course they would. They would probably be relieved to see you do it.'

I wondered why I could not grieve like everybody else and why I had an exaggerated sense of responsibility. The stigma of the murder caused me to withdraw from people. I was still inactive socially. The fact that people avoided the topic of Shirree's death eroded my normal confidence in social situations. Where I was usually able to interact comfortably with people in the past, there was now a distinct withdrawal.

Brad was in the same position. He continued to tough it out, mostly alone. I was proud of my son. Whatever decisions I made, Brad was one hundred per cent behind me. Brad didn't want any attention so I encouraged him to stay in the background but there was a desperate little boy behind the protective brick wall he'd built around himself. I could empathise with my son because I had built the same tall wall around myself.

There were times when I felt I may have taken on more than I could cope with although it never occurred to me that I wouldn't go ahead with the civil action. I'd heard somewhere that if you want something badly enough you should find out how, then just do it.

Dr Williams listened to my fears and gave helpful advice. She prescribed medication and although I didn't like to take tablets I was grateful at times for the temporary relief they gave. The underlying problems were still with me. My health issue was a time bomb ticking away.

Chapter 15
Media Attention

The sun came out after an early shower, preserving the freshness of the morning. It was a typical spring day promising warm sunshine. My mood was bright with anticipation. The film crew for *A Current Affair* were expected early.

Mike Munro called from the airport asking me to meet the team at police headquarters. 'I want to get an interview if possible but they don't know we're coming so I'm not sure how we'll be received. After that, I think we'll go to Oaklands Park while the weather holds.'

'That sounds okay. I'm leaving the house now.'

'Is it still okay to do the bulk of the interview with you at the house?'

'Yes. What time do you think you'll be here?'

'I'd say about eleven or twelve. But don't hold me to that. It depends on the cops and the weather.'

'It won't matter. Lesley will be here. She's my assistant. She's happy for you to do whatever you need when we get here.'

'Great. I'll see you soon.'

Shirree's friend, Sonia, had graciously agreed to be interviewed and it was decided to film her at night in Hindley Street. Mike and the team were very professional about their work. They were fortunate to secure a brief interview with Superintendent Trevor Johnson. The police were reluctant to grant the interview but Mike was very persuasive.

I drove Mike to the Oaklands Park Reserve while the rest of the team followed in the hire car. Filming took place in the reserve, at the house where Shirree was found, outside the apartment block where Mercuri had lived and on Marion Road where the handbags were found.

At the house the crew carried out sound and lighting tests while Mike explained how he wanted the interview to go. 'I want you to relax and answer the questions calmly and honestly. We'll cover a lot of ground but it will be edited. Be natural; be yourself. If you make a mistake, don't worry. We'll be doing several takes of some questions.'

The interview process was easier said than done. After several hours my interview was complete and the team headed to Hindley Street for Sonia's interview. The *ACA* team were then going to Melbourne to interview the young woman whom Mercuri attacked on New Year's Eve 1994. They wanted to give Mercuri a chance to have his say but were not confident of gaining an interview with him.

Several days after filming, Leonie Dale and a photographer from *Woman's Day* came to interview me for the magazine article. There was an anxious wait for news to be aired and the magazine article to be published.

To keep busy in the interim I had letters written to politicians and key people, lobbying for changes to Similar Fact Evidence laws and what constituted admissible evidence.

On 11 September 1998 Morry was ready to personally deliver the first documents stating that I, Ken Turner, intended to sue Frank Mercuri for the wrongful death of my daughter. At the same time, Frank Mercuri was served with documents asking him to prove his innocence in another court. This time he would be required to provide some evidence of his innocence because the burden of proof was not so much in his favour. It would not be as easy for him to sit back and allow a lawyer to weave a defence. During the entire lead-up to the civil action Frank Mercuri was never available to receive documents personally. In almost all instances, according to affidavits supplied by process servers, either a parent or grandparent signed for the papers.

I was informed that the story for *A Current Affair* was to be screened on Tuesday 15 September. For several days prior, promotional advertisements saturated the airwaves. The magazine article in *Woman's Day* was set for release the same week. Television advertising for the magazine used the story as a feature and I couldn't wait to see both stories.

Front-page headlines in *The Advertiser* for Monday 14 September read, 'Father sues man cleared of murder'.[10] The article went on to say, 'In civil proceedings which bear similarities to the OJ Simpson case in the United States, Mr Turner will rely on the balance of probabilities rather than the higher test of proving guilt beyond a reasonable doubt which applies in criminal cases. Mercuri's previous convictions including one for the attempted rape and stabbing of a young woman, may also be admissible.'

On Tuesday 15 September another article was published with the headline 'Flashbacks to a nightmare', with a by-line reading, 'Murdered victim's father tells of trauma'.[11] The article stated that copies of the court documents told of the reasons for the civil action. 'In what is believed to be Australia's first wrongful death suit, Mr Turner is suing the man acquitted of [Shirree's] murder.'

The report traced the trauma and subsequent suffering I had endured since my daughter's death. 'They say the plaintiff continues to suffer symptoms of post-traumatic stress disorder and depression, manifesting partly in flashbacks of images and scenes to which he was exposed on June 6 and 7, 1993, as well as insomnia and nightmares ... Mr Turner's shock and depression worsened when the not guilty verdict was returned.'

A second article was published under the headline 'Attempted rape conviction "pertinent" to case'.[12] It stated that the attempted rape case was most pertinent to the civil action. It was reported Mercuri was now out of jail on parole.

I purchased several copies of *Woman's Day*, which was released early on the Tuesday morning, and was delighted with the article written by Leonie Dale. She concentrated on the story from my point of view as a grieving father, shattered by the acquittal and fighting for justice for my only daughter.

Titled 'Australia's First OJ Simpson Trial'[13], the article stated I was not vengeful or carrying on a vendetta and was certainly not obsessed. Leonie reported my outrage that elements of the defendant's criminal past could not be included in the trial and that Shirree's murder had taken an obvious toll on my health. Reasons why Shirree's death had affected me were also listed.

'Now I've been robbed of so many things. I will never be able to walk my beautiful daughter down the aisle when she gets married ... And I'll never be able to have grandchildren by her marriage because some incompetent man took her life in a very violent way.'

Leonie concluded the article with a quote from Shirree's diary. 'My goal is to find the right guy. I also want to have a beautiful wedding day full of love and a romantic honeymoon ... Also, just as important are children. I will love them just as much, and we will be a really nice family together.' I could not have been more pleased. The article explained just how life had changed for me since Shirree's death. Leonie didn't miss a thing and interpreted my feelings exactly.

On the same day the story aired on *A Current Affair*.[14] The short report told how I wanted only justice, not money, because I felt the justice system let my family down. The report included an interview with Mercuri's 1994 victim. It started with details of Shirree's murder and an interview with her friend Sonia. Sonia told Mike Munro that she and Kirsty had left Shirree for a quick dance to a favourite song.

'What was the last thing you said to her?' Mike Munro asked.

'Could you mind our handbags?' Sonia replied sadly.

'And you never saw her again?' Mike Munro probed. Sonia shook her head slowly, unable to speak. Mike continued the report, filling in details of the crime and how the criminal trial had progressed. I watched as the focus of the interview returned to me.

'Mr Turner, let me put these points to you. No eyewitnesses to the murder. No evidence as to how Shirree got to Oaklands Park or who with. No murder weapon has ever been found. There's no motive and no forensic evidence linking Shirree with Frank Mercuri? Now, they're all pretty compelling reasons to acquit him?'

'Yes,' I replied, 'but I still go back to the fact that if the true nature of Frank Mercuri was allowed to be used in the criminal justice system then the jury would have seen the true character of this man.'

Mike Munro looked into the camera. 'The jury was never allowed to know during the trial that Frank Mercuri was arriving each day in court from jail. He was still serving a term for the attempted rape and stabbing of another young woman ... this young woman.' The camera panned to the young woman who for the purposes of this interview was to be called Caroline. She described the night that Mercuri attacked her.

'He [Mercuri] just kept smiling at me like it was some kind of big joke ... like ... it's almost as though what he was doing wasn't anything serious ... you know ... it was ...' Caroline hesitated.

'Smiling?' Mike Munro asked in disbelief.

Caroline continued bravely, 'I saw evil in his eyes.'

'What did you think Mercuri ultimately wanted to do to you?' Mike Munro probed.

'I thought he was going to kill me.'

Mike went on to report that eighteen months after Shirree's murder, on New Year's Eve 1994, Caroline agreed to have a drink with her 'friend' Frank Mercuri at his hotel. She'd known him for six years but had no idea about his criminal history.

The interview showed a still shot of the motel where Caroline had been attacked. 'The knife came out ... he stabbed me about four times I'd say ... in the arm first and then ... he proceeded to try to ... er ... try to rape me ... but couldn't ... and then he just went mad.'

'How many times altogether did he stab you?' Mike Munro asked.

Caroline replied, almost in tears, 'Seven times. Twice in the chest ... five times in the arm.'

'Somehow Caroline managed to break free from the first floor room and ran down a flight of stairs, only to have Mercuri drag her back up and throw her off the balcony,' Mike continued.

'The anger, the aggression ... the way I saw him come after me ... I'd say he'd have no problem doing it to someone he didn't know.'

Mike went on to explain that apart from Caroline's horrific case, the law also prevented the Shirree Turner jury from knowing about Mercuri's forty-eight previous convictions in Victoria, which included attempted armed robbery, recklessly causing injury, and dishonesty. Nor was it privy to his South Australian conviction.

My face returned to the TV screen as I said, 'I believe that Frank Mercuri murdered my daughter Shirree. It's my belief that if the jury, the members of the jury, had known the true character of Frank Mercuri, it would have thrown a whole new light on the situation.'

'But you and I both know that that's the justice system ... that we can't contaminate a case with past convictions,' Mike argued.

'I understand that is true, but I think in some cases the true character of that person needs to be bought out to enable a jury to make a fair verdict,' I explained.

'Unlike criminal trials, Ken Turner's landmark civil action will allow Mercuri's full criminal history to be admitted into evidence before the Judge. Ken Turner is not just doing this for his daughter; he's doing it for other young woman ... like Caroline.'

Caroline's face was shown briefly as she said, 'You move on ... but you take it with you. Now, things are better for me ... you know. But I know

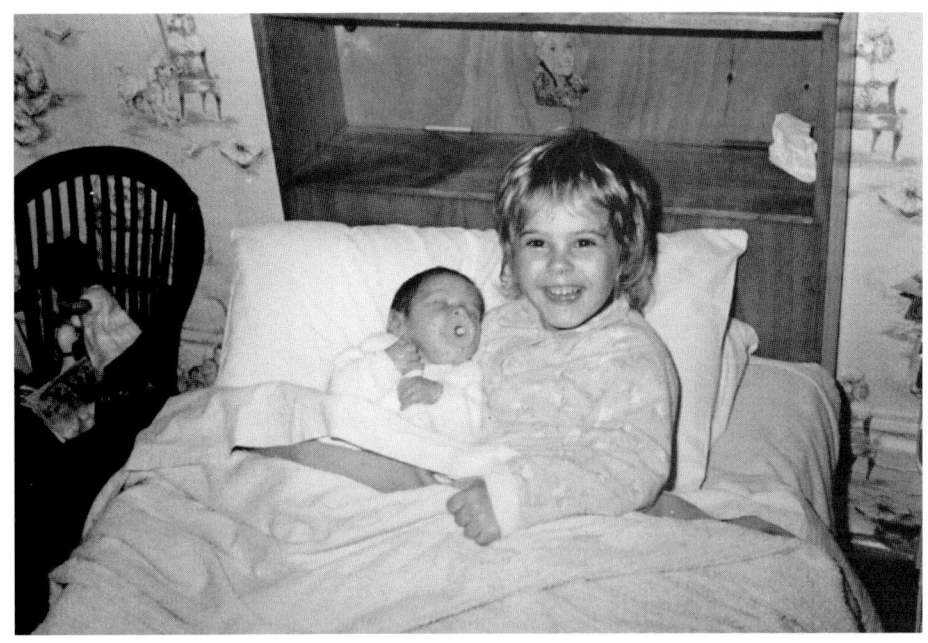

Shirree cuddles her baby brother, Bradley, soon after he was born.

Ready to party — Shirree aged 6, with Bradley aged 4.

Shirree, aged 3, with Bradley on his 1st birthday.

Shirree with Bradley on her 21st brithday.

Shiree's school photo —
ribbons and curls she was
daddy's little girl.

Christmas 1978 —
Shirree was proud of her
new bike.

Shirree and Fabio were very happy in the early days.

Shirree holidaying in Melbourne with friends when she was 18 years old.

SHIRREE: A loving life that ended in tragedy

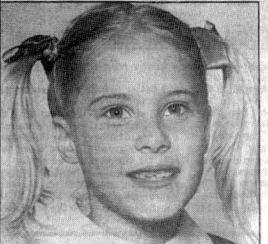

Pretty in ponytails in a school photograph.

One of the last photos of Shirree at 22.

By Police Reporter
LESLEY JOHNS

At her fourth birthday party.

With father Ken on her 16th birthday.

They are like countless family snapshots the world over ... the baby photo, the birthday parties, the playtime pictures, the student in uniform.

They are the photos that follow the life of Shirree Ann Turner as a bubbly blonde schoolgirl grows into a smiling young woman.

But for Shirree, life ended prematurely, brutally, after only 22 years.

In the dark hours of Sunday morning the child-care worker from Brooklyn Park died of multiple stab wounds to the chest.

They were inflicted during what apparently was a violent sexual assault in Oaklands Reserve, in the southern suburb of Oaklands Park.

As her life ebbed away, Shirree struggled out of the reserve and into Minchinbury Tce to seek help. But the house she crawled to was unoccupied.

It was 8am before a neighbor found her body slumped on the porch.

She was last seen alive, and alone, walking west along Hindley St in the city, between midnight and 1am, wearing a black evening dress and carrying three handbags — her own and those of two friends.

The bags were found about 2km from the murder scene.

Police, still seeking a breakthrough in their investigations, appealed last night for a man who has made two phone calls about the murder to contact them on 207 5412.

The man first called the police 000 emergency number several days ago and made a second call to the Channel 7 newsroom last night.

Detectives said last night they needed to talk to him again. They have guaranteed to keep his information confidential.

"Community safety is at risk; we've got a murderer out there and the quicker we get him off the streets the better," a police spokesman said.

Senior police have described the manner in which Shirree was killed as horrendous.

"She was set upon viciously and cruelly," a police source said.

"He (the killer) stripped her of dignity and it's quite obvious by the injuries that she did everything she could to

Enjoying a boat ride in the family pool, aged about seven.

maintain that dignity — she put up a brave fight."

Family and friends described Shirree, who would have turned 23 on July 22, as an "outdoors girl" who loved the beach and played netball and softball.

"She had two goals — to be happy and to one day settle down and have a family," said her grieving father, former pastor Mr Ken Turner. "At least she achieved one of those goals.

"The love in her heart was immense. She cared about people and they cared about her.

"Even as a young child she was always surrounded by dozens of kids."

That magnetism for children had been with Shirree since she was a youngster. She had wanted for a long time to make a career of working with children.

When she completed her schooling at Underdale High School she worked part-time as a receptionist while she studied for a child-care certificate.

Her dedication paid off and she eventually was employed as a child-care worker.

Shirree had a remarkably wide circle of friends. One of her closest was 22-year-old Gjuzide Zeneli, who wrote the poem on this page as a tribute.

"She was always there," Gjuzide said. "If anybody ever needed anything, she would give it."

● PAGE 11: Major crime squads fully stretched
● PAGE 22: Editorial

Memories of Shirree in *The Advertiser* 12 June 1993.

Goodbye Shirree — Lena, one of Shirree's closest friends expresses the grief felt by mourners at Shirree's funeral, from *The Advertiser* 17 June 1993.

Exposed: the dark side of Frank Mercuri

By Court Reporter
FIONA CLARK

FRANK Mercuri – acquitted this week of murdering Shirree Turner in 1993 – is back in jail for stabbing and attempting to rape a Victorian woman in 1994.

The 26-year-old has hardly seen the outside of a prison since he was 19.

After the Adelaide trial ended, he was returned to the Barwon prison in Geelong to serve the tail end of a sentence for attempted rape and intentionally causing serious injury.

Mercuri was sentenced in the Melbourne County Court in 1995 to four years with a minimum term of 33 months.

He will be eligible to apply for parole in August this year.

On New Year's Eve, 1994, Mercuri – recently released from prison – had been catching up and drinking with friends.

He invited a woman friend back to his motel room for a drink before telling her he had always wanted to kiss her.

He then pulled out a kitchen knife and pushed it into the woman's shoulder until she bled.

● Continued Page 2

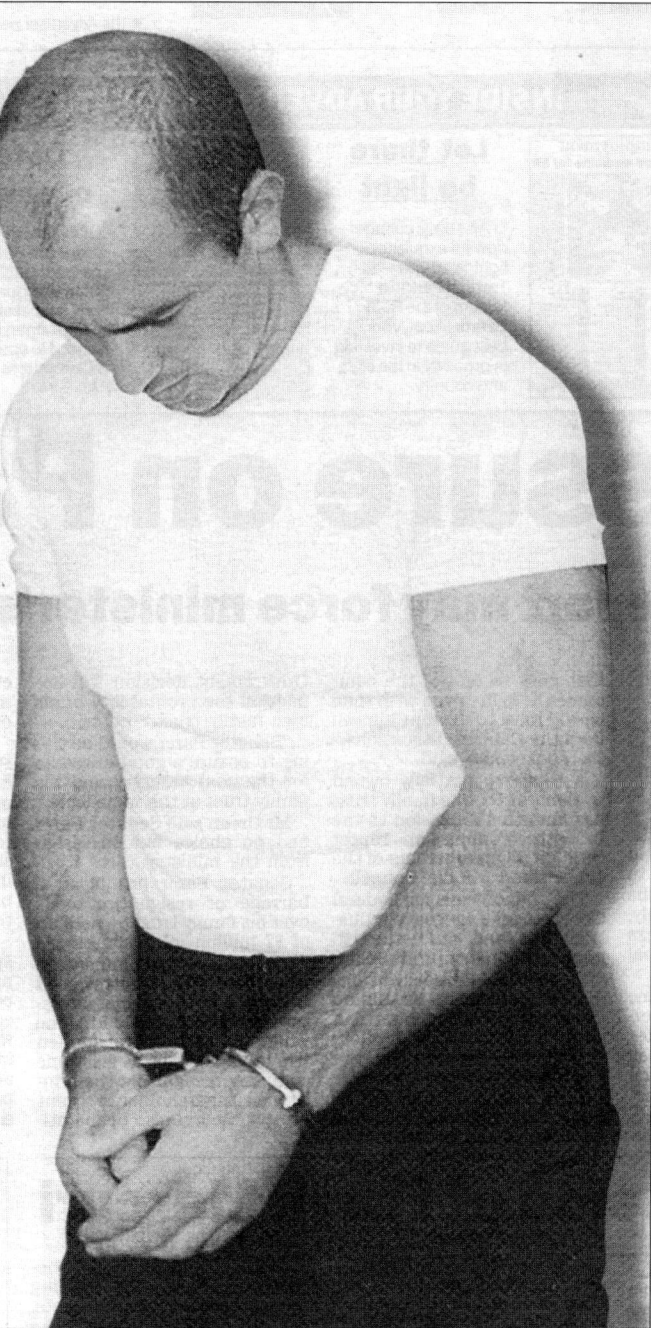

The jury was unaware of Mercuri's criminal past, from *The Advertiser* 21 March 1998.

Father who wanted justice finds peace

Ken was able to move on with his life at last, newspaper clipping from *The Advertiser* 12 October 1999.

Civil suit over Shirree's murder dropped

By Court Reporter
MICHAEL OWEN-BROWN

DESPITE being forced by ill-health to drop a civil lawsuit against the man he believes killed his daughter, Ken Turner says he is finally at peace.

In a South Australian legal first, Turner had sued Frank Mercuri, the man acquitted of murdering his daughter, Shirree Turner.

Ms Turner was stabbed five times in a reserve in Oaklands Park June, 1993.

Mercuri last year was found not guilty of murdering Ms Turner, 22, but Mr Turner launched civil proceedings alleging Mercuri was responsible for her wrongful death.

He was disappointed that legal restrictions meant the jury was not told Mercuri had 48 convictions, including a stabbing and attempted rape.

But yesterday, on the first morn-

"Even though she's gone to be in heaven, I feel peaceful, I feel warm inside . . . free to start a whole new life and put all this behind me."

Mr Turner will continue to campaign for previous convictions and similar-fact evidence to be admissible as evidence in jury trials. He said not allowing such evidence meant juries were only seeing part of the picture.

"I'm very disappointed in the criminal justice system," he said.

"In due course they'll have no option but to change the law because of what it's doing to our society."

> ❛ I feel like a big burden has been lifted from my life ❜

it's something that is always going to be there ... you know ... like I said ... I just need to look at my scars every day.'

Mike Munro concluded the report. 'Frank Mercuri declined to be interviewed. He says he's innocent and a jury has already cleared him of murder. Now he has to decide whether to defend that civil action brought by Ken Turner and we'll keep watching the case.'

It was over. I breathed a sigh of relief. I felt the story had been brilliantly done and could not have been happier. I knew Caroline had consented to be interviewed but I had not seen the interview before this. I'd spoken to her by phone but had not met this very brave young woman. I was so proud of her.

Shortly after the screening of *A Current Affair* Mike Munro called with news about ratings. It disturbed me that the show rated much higher in the eastern states. In light of the publicity the story received in the days leading up to the screening, I was surprised and disappointed in the lack of interest shown in Adelaide. Were the public apathetic or just plain embarrassed about the number of murders, particularly stabbing murders, occurring in Adelaide?

Another surprise was on the way. A week after the screening I received a call from the program's producer, John McAvoy. A viewer had been sufficiently moved by the story and contacted the program wanting to be put in touch with me. 'I'm happy for you to give him my mobile phone number, John. I'd like to hear what he has to say if you think it would be a good idea.'

'He sounded genuinely concerned, Ken. I don't think it would hurt to talk to him. I'll contact him and pass on your number. Keep in touch though and let me know if there is anything that I can do.'

A few days later the man, who will be known as Jonathon (to protect his identity) called. Jonathon had daughters of his own. He described his outrage at Shirree's murder and also what I was going through because of the outcome of the criminal trial. He was amazed by Caroline's courage in telling her story and spoke of his disgust at the inadequate sentence handed down by the court. Jonathon also felt that the courts had become far too lenient on violent offenders, especially repeat offenders.

Jonathon said he would have been just as devastated if anything happened to one of his daughters. He encouraged me to continue the pursuit of justice, saying he would like to help in some practical way if I would allow him to do so. I was in no position to refuse.

Jonathon wanted to help finance the legal costs for the civil action. I was astounded at the substantial sum he offered. I could hardly believe that a stranger, unconnected in any way to my family, was willing to help financially. I didn't know what to say; I was so overwhelmed by his generosity.

During the build-up to the civil action Jonathon and I kept in regular contact. I was concerned about mounting legal costs. There had already been delays and this was a worry but I believed wholeheartedly the costs would be covered somehow or I would be able to pay off any balance over time if necessary.

Tindall, Gask & Bentley were very generous in trimming costs to a bare minimum. I had been quoted sums of between $50,000 and $80,000 to provide a legal service for a civil action of this nature.

Chapter 16

Politics and the Law

The deadline for a response from Mercuri to defend the civil action came and went with no word of what his intention might be. Proof of service documents were lodged with the District Court and my hopes began to rise. It looked like Mercuri might decide not to defend the action, in which case judgment would be made in my favour and the case could be listed for assessment of damages.

Then finally, Mercuri lodged documents stating he had every intention of defending the claims. His excuse for the late lodgment was his difficulty in obtaining legal advice. Notification was received from a law firm in Adelaide who were acting as agents for Mercuri's lawyer in Melbourne. They requested a further twenty-eight days to prepare and file proper documents. They reasoned that the solicitor who was to prepare the documents was out of state on another case.

'Ken, any lawyer could have filed the documents. I've given them until the close of court on 9 October. I've told them that failure to file means we'll seek a judgment and a listing for assessment of damages.' The documents were filed before the second deadline.

Morry received a letter from Mercuri through a solicitor from the Legal Services Commission of South Australia dated 14 October. They requested the hearing for judgment that was on 29 October be vacated as Mercuri intended to appear in person and was still trying to get legal assistance from legal services. Legal aid had been refused.

'He'll try to delay proceedings as long as he can, Ken. My guess is he'll try to get you to give up and drop the action.' It appeared the battle lines had been drawn and delay tactics had started.

The Advertiser updated the case under the headline 'Denial on killing'.[15] In the report, Mercuri denied I had any entitlement to damages. In the documents filed in his defence he denied responsibility for Shirree's death and therefore liability for damages. Civil law states that an action must be commenced within three years of the event, in this case Shirree's murder. Mercuri claimed that I had satisfied none of the grounds for an extension of time to instigate proceedings outside of the normal statutory limitations for a civil action. I was advised an application for an extension of time in this case would be successful if it could be established there was a material fact altering the plaintiff's circumstances. That fact was well established; the criminal trial was not completed until almost five years after the murder.

A medical report established that my health worsened dramatically after Mercuri's acquittal. Together with the time lapse between the murder and the court trial it was enough to establish grounds for an extension. My doctor described the nature and extent the acquittal was having on my physical and psychological wellbeing as both immediate and long term.

Morry wasn't happy with the document purporting to be Mercuri's defence. In his opinion the document was deficient. Mercuri hadn't attended any hearings nor had he appointed a legal representative. It was a breach of District Court rules. Late in October, Morry applied for Mercuri's defence to be struck out and for our claims to be listed for assessment. A hearing scheduled for late November was adjourned and rescheduled for 10 December. More delays.

Morry appeared before the Master of the Court. Again Mercuri did not attend. It was pointed out to Master Berry that it was the second occasion the defendant hadn't appeared. Master Berry referred to a letter stating Mercuri could not get legal aid but wanted to defend the action. Master Berry ordered the defendant to comply with certain conditions and listed the action for a conciliation conference before a Short Notice Judge.

It was frustrating. My lawyers and I were being thwarted by the system again. Hearings were deferred, rescheduled and adjourned while Masters and Judges scurried back to law books. The case was the first of its kind in Australia and there was no precedent to refer to.

I felt that Mercuri's rights were given more consideration than mine were. He continued to flout the rules of the District Court using every trick in the book. I wondered what the outcome would be if the case was an accident or some other minor offence. I felt there would have been no hesitation in handing down a swift judgment and the case would have been over in a matter of weeks.

There was little happening over the Christmas break. Morry wrote to Jonathon updating him on the trial proceedings or lack thereof. Morry was quietly confident that if Mercuri did not appear in court the next time, or at least be represented, a judgment might be entered. Even if Mercuri did appear, Morry anticipated a listing for trial.

During January 1999 several hearings took place. Preparation for the trial continued even though it looked likely that Mercuri would decide not to continue with his defence. Mercuri was experiencing difficulty, conditions of his parole were creating problems for him.

Late in January 1999 Morry lodged documents about my health problems, which had considerably worsened. The doctors documented in a series of comprehensive reports my entire health history since the murder in 1993. The reply to the defence was filed at the same time.

Mercuri had lodged documents which again we felt were deficient. He was still not complying with court directives.

Mercuri called Morry in early February stating he was making an application to adjourn the next scheduled case evaluation conference. 'I anticipate that my client will oppose that application,' Morry responded.

'Why?' Mercuri asked.

'I am not at liberty, nor under any obligation to explain why,' Morry replied. 'It would be far better if you could see your way clear to attend in person or at least appoint a representative' was all the advice Morry intended giving Mercuri.

'I don't think I can do that.'

'I am sorry then. It would be most inappropriate for me to comment any further. It is really a matter for you to work out for yourself.'

Mercuri was notified by letter, that in the context of case-flow and in fairness to the plaintiff, it was unreasonable to delay proceedings until after his parole expired. It was further stated that Master Berry's orders from 10 December must be adhered to. Notification was given to Mercuri and the conference was adjourned until 25 March. The notification stated that the plaintiff would be seeking orders to expedite the finalisation of his claim.

The Judge hinted that on the next occasion there couldn't be any conceivable excuse for the defendant to ignore the situation and not comply with court orders. The advice given intimated that if Mercuri continued to ignore the court orders it would be reasonable to presume the matter would be listed for trial.

The next hearing date was adjourned. Master Berry took some time to consider the application before making a ruling. It was back to the law books. My lawyers had presented another dilemma for Master Berry. On the evening before the decision on our application was handed down, *A Current Affair* updated the story.

Morry said that we'd had some difficulty with Mercuri's defence and would make an application to strike it out. 'If the application is granted on this occasion the matter will then be listed for assessment of damages. Apart from that it will be listed for trial in the future,' Morry said.

'If Frank Mercuri is still not represented at tomorrow's hearing, Ken Turner and his lawyers hope to claim victory in the civil case,' Mike Munro reported.

'It's definitely a good sign. It shows he is weakening. He's obviously having difficulty in getting somebody to defend him and yes, we feel there is a victory just around the corner,' I stated, trying not to sound overconfident.

The following day Master Berry handed down his decision. In a document stating his reasons for deciding as he did, Master Berry gave all of the facts relating to Mercuri's non-compliance to the court's previous orders. He stated that despite the fact that Mercuri had not complied with the court orders, he had at least been in touch with the Court from time to time. Master Berry stated Mercuri seemed to be in a position of some difficulty but that I was entitled to have my claim proceed in compliance with case-flow management. Master Berry could see no basis for the action to be delayed until Mercuri's parole conditions expired.

However, despite all of the facts, Master Berry decided that striking out Mercuri's defence would result in an injustice to the defendant. He directed the appropriate ruling would be to list the action for an early trial. The matter was adjourned, placing the action on the court docket for trial as early as possible. The defendant was to be notified of the trial date by letter.

I was disappointed the court glossed over my feelings yet again and seemed to bend over backwards for Mercuri. I understood the difficulties Mercuri was having but I faced difficulties as well. The uncertainty and delays continued to take a huge toll on my health and although I was able to hide my emotions, inside I was a mess. The worry over whether Mercuri was using delay tactics to wear me down only created a firmer resolve to keep going. But when was enough going to be enough?

Morry and Brendan were concerned about my increasing lack of energy and enthusiasm. They could see through the facade and so could my friends and family. Morry and I talked about Master Berry's decision and decided to make an appeal. An appeal wouldn't cause a delay and might benefit us. In any event, we were prepared to take the chance.

Morry worked long hours on the appeal on the grounds that insufficient weight was given to Mercuri's non-compliance with court directives. The plaintiff wanted justice to be applied appropriately, as would be granted in a civil action for any other offence. In our opinion, special consideration should not be given just because an action of this type had not been tried before. The same rules should apply for every case. Non-compliance with court directives would have been harshly dealt with in other situations. We felt that we were entitled to the same consideration.

Morry and Brendan continued with the trial preparation so they would be ready for all contingencies. Their feeling was cautiously guarded about whether Mercuri would show up at the trial. His track record for non-appearance so far indicated there was a strong possibility he wouldn't appear or be represented. This thought kept alive the glimmer of hope for justice that I had clung to for so long.

On 18 May, ten days before the appeal, Michael Owen-Brown wrote a beautiful article in *The Advertiser* under the headline 'God's gift to me'. The byline read, 'Why Ken Turner fights for justice over the murder of his daughter'.[16] The report explored my reasons for instigating the civil action. Michael wanted to incorporate an in-depth story about my relationship with Shirree and how the criminal trial verdict had an ongoing effect on my state of mind. I gave Michael a different photograph of Shirree to use with the article. It was one of my favourite photographs, taken on her twenty-first birthday.

I stated I was motivated by lingering feelings of the injustice dealt to me by the acquittal of the accused murderer. I was still convinced, without any shadow of doubt, that Mercuri was the culprit. It was reported that I was lobbying the State Government in an attempt to have Similar Fact Evidence admissible in trials where the evidence could make a difference.

'I can't see how anybody can make the right decision without knowing all of the facts,' I stated. 'You can't delete the character of a criminal when he's been accused of such a horrendous crime as murder ... I feel that if I don't pursue this to the end then I will never be able to rest ... If we can start a precedent for other things to help the criminal justice system then it will make a better community for us to live in and maybe our sons and daughters will be safer on the streets.'

I reiterated that I was not criticising the criminal justice system but believed some reforms were required. 'The truth is what will set me free,' I stated. 'My beautiful daughter was God's gift to me.'

On 10 May Judge Kitchen heard the appeal. Morry argued that Master Berry's refusal to strike out the defence be overruled on grounds that Mercuri hadn't attended pre-trial hearings or been represented. Morry stated they would have to issue subpoenas for many witnesses and pointed out it would be unjust to subject the plaintiff to the expense when the defendant might not show up at trial. Our argument included Mercuri's non-compliance with document filing rules and the fact that Mercuri hadn't given adequate contact details as directed by the court.

Judge Kitchen disagreed the trial would not be fair to the plaintiff. Again I felt frustrated that Mercuri was being given more of a fair deal than would be given another defendant. It was obvious we were not going to be successful so Morry withdrew the appeal. I had to face the disappointment and frustration that can only be felt when injustice prevails. Once again the court bent over backwards to accommodate Mercuri and although I knew the Judge would not agree, the trial should have been over months ago. I did not think I was being fairly treated compared to plaintiffs in other civil actions.

I felt I was being penalised for Mercuri's mistakes. Was it my fault Mercuri was unable to attend hearings? Was it my fault Mercuri could not obtain representation? Mercuri was not even complying with court directives. What did I have to do to be granted a fair hearing? Why couldn't the court see that Mercuri was doing all he could to stall for time?

In May 1999 a hearing was listed to set a trial date for 11 October. It was estimated that five days would be needed to hear the evidence. Ironically, the new trial date was the day after Mercuri's parole was due to expire.

I was pleased that at last a date had been set but I had five more months to wait. I thought about getting out of Adelaide for a while because my health was declining rapidly. In an attempt to reverse the situation I made tentative plans to return to Noosa for a short vacation.

To take the civil action to trial, Morry engaged the services of Andrew Martin QC, a well-respected barrister who agreed to act on my behalf. During May all documentation regarding the case was transferred to Martin's office. For the next few weeks there would be no more court involvement and no need for any more conferences until just before the October trial date.

I found I had to put my plans for a holiday on hold for a few weeks, however. I had been working on a testimony that I hoped to share in schools and youth groups and needed to generate some financial back-up. I decided to apply for a grant offered by the National Bank Community Link Awards. I needed references from two prominent members of the community and there were none more prominent than Steve Condous. Steve was a local member of parliament whom I had met during the police investigation in 1993.

I hadn't seen Steve for some time so I brought him up to date with the civil action including details about Mercuri's past. Steve became an ally expressing real concern and asked me to collate the data about Similar Fact Evidence laws and my subsequent disappointment in the justice system. He also wanted details about Mercuri's criminal history.

Steve promised that if I could provide details and documents to back up my concerns then he would raise the issue in parliament, hopefully sparking some interest in the right places. Steve was very concerned about the way in which criminals were able to circumvent the system and were either getting away with crimes or receiving only minor penalties for serious charges.

'I think a periodic review of the law would make the system more equitable. Criminals should be made more accountable for their actions. I'm in favour of stronger deterrents and I'd also like to see better rehabilitation programs implemented,' I told him. 'You know, Steve, repeat offenders have a sound knowledge of how the system works and what their "rights" are. It gives them an edge on beating the system. There doesn't seem to be any incentive for crims to rehabilitate themselves.'

Steve agreed in principle with my viewpoint. He echoed most of my concerns for the justice system. He was aware of the groundswell of discontent in the community. 'You're right. At least if a periodic review was conducted the system would not appear to be stagnating.'

I was amazed at the way Steve took on the concerns I had raised. Steve was a family man and could identify with what I was going through. He was keen to add his weight as an MP on the backbench to help gain some ground in the fight against injustice for victims. I left his office with a profound sense of gratitude for his interest in the cause and headed home to begin the task of collating the relevant data.

I made a decision to return to Noosa Heads for a vacation in the second week of August. I intended to spend at least five weeks away. My estimated return was planned for mid-September. I felt it would give me some much-needed rest before the trial, yet still allow enough time to visit Dr Williams for a final report on my state of health. I also needed to have time to spend with Morry and Andrew Martin to make certain they had all the information needed to take the action to court.

After Morry approved the material I handed on to Steve, he then delivered his speech on my behalf in the South Australian State Parliament during a night sitting. The speech was filmed for the television news and it caused quite a stir.

Also that night, Nick Colquhoun reported the speech for Channel Nine's 6 pm news program. He related that an accusation of a brutal murder had been levelled at the acquitted man. It was also suspected he was responsible for the death of a six-year-old boy, almost exactly twelve months after Shirree was murdered. Nick described how, in an extraordinary speech before State Parliament, the Liberal backbencher had named Mercuri as being responsible for the death of the boy in a house fire in 1994. Steve accused Mercuri of picking up the boy's mother from a city nightclub and taking her home where, because of an impotence problem, he allegedly got frustrated and angry and set fire to the house ,resulting in the boy's death.

Nick reported the allegation was contained in the speech that also criticised current laws believed responsible for Mercuri walking free of Shirree's murder. The report revealed again that before and after the trial Mercuri had spent time in a Victorian prison for an almost identical crime. 'But the jury was never told at the time because under South Australian law a defendant's criminal history is inadmissible, a situation Steve Condous wants changed,' Nick recounted.

'The law in this particular case is an ass,' Steve had stated. Nick finished his report by stating the police identified a suspect during the investigation into the house fire but would not confirm if it was Mercuri. Police stated charges were never laid because of a lack of evidence and with the death of the boy's mother that status was unlikely to change.

I was very pleased the issues I raised with Steve had finally been brought into the open. However, it still remained to be seen whether the events would stir any interest from the government, and even then if they would act on the issues.

The morning after the speech an editorial was published in *The Advertiser* under the headline, 'A difficult question of judgment'.[17] Comments by the editor presented a balanced view of what Steve had raised in Parliament:

Steve Condous reminded us of the value of backbenchers and the positive side of parliamentary privilege in a speech in the House of Assembly.

He referred to a celebrated South Australian case in which the person charged was acquitted by a jury in a verdict with which the judge concurred, saying it was entirely proper.

Speaking on behalf of Mr Ken Turner, whose daughter Shirree, 22, was murdered in 1993, Mr Condous noted that Frank Mercuri, the man charged, had 48 previous convictions for violent crime. His and Mr Turner's contention is that judges and juries said the law should be changed to allow judges and juries to be aware of previous convictions.

The only clear issue in this instance is Mr Turner's understandable continuing grief and distress. He has our utmost sympathy while Mr Condous himself performed a small public service by canvassing the matter.

The MP makes a case, which is perhaps worthy of being informally further canvassed by the Attorney-General on behalf of the Government, his Opposition shadow and the judiciary.

A criminal record, especially one involving possibly relevant offences, may, indeed, be pertinent.

Yet ultimately, the very cornerstone of our system, derived from English law, is the presumption of innocence. Raising previous convictions may impute guilt and therefore be unacceptable. This is a serious objection.

Two weeks later, the Attorney-General issued a circular[18] to all Liberal members of parliament at a Liberal Party meeting about the admissibility of previous convictions in criminal trials. In a covering note the Attorney-General stated the issue had been raised in the joint party room, and details of the current law pertaining to the issue were attached. It was also stated at the joint party meeting that any member who wished to put the matter back on the agenda could do so but would need to detail their thoughts on any alternative measures.

The Attorney-General thought that the law on the subject was not as simple as Steve Condous suggested. The very complex reasons for the law were explained. All issues pointed to the presumption of innocence that those versed in law agreed was fundamental to the criminal justice system. Moreover, it was still an integral part of criminal justice.

Summarising his view, the Attorney-General stated that just because a person had been convicted of rape in the past doesn't mean he is more likely to be guilty of rape when charged in the present. Steve Condous used an example in his speech that if a dog had bitten people in the past it was quite likely the same dog was responsible for biting a current complainant. The situation was untrue and would logically depend on other surrounding evidence. It could be a vindictive neighbour who might not be telling the truth about the dog, it might be the wrong colour or the dog might have been at the beach at the time of the complaint. There could be any number of other reasons why the dog may be wrongly accused.

The circular stated that a detailed research project into jury deliberations had found the admission of previous convictions did in fact increase the chance of a guilty verdict. However, it was only if the convictions were for offences similar to the current charge. If previous convictions were not of a similar nature then the juries tended to favour the innocence of the accused.

The Attorney-General was therefore of the opinion that the law as it had developed had the balance right, not only as a matter of law, or a matter of legal principle, but also as a matter of straightforward logic. His conclusion was that the law should not be changed.[18]

I was disappointed. In my opinion consideration was not given to both sides of the equation. The presumption of innocence argument would always be a stumbling block and was still very one-sided. Were a victim's rights or feelings ever going to be considered? No matter which way you looked at the law it was always going to consider an offender's rights before consideration of a victim's feelings. The victim, it seemed, was always going to serve a life sentence with little satisfaction in most cases.

On doctor's advice I left Adelaide for a break. I couldn't remove the thought that I was in store for another huge disappointment. It was hoped that time away from Adelaide would dispel my fears and give me a more optimistic view.

Chapter 17

Halfway to Justice

I enjoyed the change of scenery in Noosa and the weather was warmer. I was able to relax, put the doubts and fears aside for a short time, while I attempted to re-charge my batteries. I knew I would be busy when the holiday was over.

In mid-August Anna Williamson of Tindall, Gask and Bentley received a call from Andrew Martin. There was a good chance Mercuri would not turn up for the trial but witnesses still had to be ready to go. He listed the order of preference for appearance of witnesses. Subpoenas were requested, issued and served. An investigator was hired to track down current addresses for the witnesses and affidavits were lodged.

Late in August, Chris John Thallas called Anna with some concerns. He didn't want to give evidence again because the 'destruction to his life and business' after testifying at previous hearings had been very hard on him. Williamson told Thallas that his oral evidence was needed and as they were 'running the trial' he would be required to appear. In a last-ditch effort he said he was concerned for the safety of family and friends and about whether the media would be present.

'Well, I'd say due to the high-profile status of the case there is every possibility the media will be extremely interested,' Anna told him. Did Thallas really expect any sympathy? Had he thought about the consequences of his actions when he kept secret what he knew about Mercuri's involvement in Shirree's murder for more than two years? Had he given any consideration to what my family or Shirree's friends had been through? Did he care that Shirree endured a degrading sexual attack, a vicious stabbing, was left to die, terrified and alone on the porch of a stranger's house? Did he care or have any consideration for the terror she must have felt as she staggered from the reserve to the doorstep for help? Would he have had an attack of conscience and come forward with his information if the police had not gone to him first? If not for the informant it was doubtful he would have given it a casual thought. He'd been forced to tell what he knew and there was reason to believe he had not told the whole story. How much more was Chris John Thallas involved in the whole scenario? He could hardly expect any sympathy under the circumstances.

Thallas was not the only one having difficulty. Scott Schinella's father had also contacted Anna to see if anything could be done to obtain an exemption for his son. Andrew Martin was informed, 'I'll need to get independent advice but since Scott Schinella's evidence is crucial, I can't see how his evidence can be excluded.'

Schinella's father implied that his son was entertaining the idea of not appearing. 'That would be a matter for him to deal with. You know the consequences of failing to obey the summons,' Andrew told Anna. 'Running scared, aren't they?'

Stephen Ponting, the Snap-on Tools representative who sold the knife to Thallas for Mercuri's birthday gift, was also reluctant to attend the court, but for more valid reasons. He was moving interstate because of an employment opportunity and was worried he might be in trouble with his new employer if he had to come back so soon after moving. Ponting said he wanted to give evidence and that he wanted to see justice done. 'I'll have a closer look at the transcript. Evidence in person by Ponting might not be necessary but I can't guarantee anything,' Andrew said. 'Is there any more?'

My faith in justice was declining. Mercuri had not retained a lawyer and although it looked unlikely he would appear at the trial I could not bank on it. If Mercuri did come and was unrepresented I felt the trial would descend into a farce. Mercuri's attempts at submitting documentation in his defence were at best amateurish. He had been getting advice from somewhere but the papers had not been submitted by any legal representative. The papers looked like Mercuri himself had prepared them. I feared that if Mercuri tried to defend himself then the trial could not be conducted with the dignity it deserved. I could not get away from the fact that no lawyer wanted to represent him. Was it because he had no means to pay, or was it because he wasn't trying? Did he think he could get the court's sympathy by being unrepresented? Discussions with the lawyers only confirmed my thoughts. 'Try to keep going if you can. It would be a great pity to cancel out now,' I was advised.

Frank Mercuri lodged documents with the District Court on 10 September requesting an adjournment. The document dated 7 September and the accompanying affidavit stated that Mercuri wanted the trial date adjourned for eight weeks. His fiancée, who was also his only form of transport because his driver's licence had been suspended, was pregnant and due to give birth in late October. Mercuri felt it would be very unsafe for her to drive. Secondly, he was still unable to leave Victoria because of restricted parole conditions.

The matter, which had been listed for 15 September, was adjourned until 21 September. Master Berry received a fax from The Salvation Army on 21 September listing several reasons why an adjournment should be granted. The documentation from a Salvation Army chaplain, obviously designed to give added weight and sympathy to Mercuri's request, contained extra considerations beside those mentioned.

Firstly, it explained how Mercuri's parole expired the day before the trial date leaving little time for him to arrange to be in Adelaide in time for the beginning of the trial. Secondly, his partner was having difficulties with the pregnancy. Thirdly, it would be difficult financially because of limited part-time work due to intensive correction order commitments. The fourth reason stated Mercuri and his partner had nowhere to stay and living in the car was not an ideal option.

Again the scheduled hearing was adjourned and finally on 30 September a telephone conference was scheduled for the next day. Anna Williamson was armed with several grounds on which we, the plaintiff, opposed the application. Anna claimed that despite the alleged default of the defendant, Master Berry had ordered on 30 March that the matter should be continued and a trial date listed following the expiration of Mercuri's parole on 10 October. Secondly, the trial date was set on 27 March. There'd been more than sufficient time for the defendant to request an adjournment. Thirdly, six witnesses were already subpoenaed and one witness arranged to attend on the first day. The fourth reason she gave was that two expert medical witnesses were booked for attendance, and Counsel, Andrew Martin was booked to attend the trial.

As a result Master Berry told Mercuri that the Salvation Army had arranged to supply bus fare and accommodation for him to come to Adelaide so Mercuri had no alternative but to drop that excuse. Mercuri complained he didn't have anybody to represent him. Mercuri had spoken to a solicitor from Legal Services in Victoria who told him the trial could not proceed because they had not supplied him with 'a hand-up brief'.

'No hand-up brief is necessary, Mr Mercuri. This is a civil matter in the civil jurisdiction of the District Court,' Master Berry replied. Mercuri said he had tried to call a legal adviser to whom he'd been referred but hadn't received a response to his messages. Master Berry noted that the Legal Services Commission had decided they would not fund Mercuri's accommodation or his bus fare but they might be willing to represent him.

Mercuri complained again that he had no way of getting to Adelaide. Master Berry reminded him the Salvation Army were prepared to provide a bus ticket and was looking into the accommodation issue. In fact they had faxed the court and were making arrangements to accommodate him. He was running out of excuses.

'As far as the application is concerned I am not disposed to take the matter out of the trial list. Arrangements have been put in place to have witnesses attend and it would cause difficulty to have the matter adjourned at this late date simply on the basis of your difficulties—difficulties which are not insurmountable.

'My ruling, therefore, is that the trial date will stand. I am offering to assist you in any way that I can. You only need to call and speak to me if you experience any more difficulties. I will assist you if I can. I will also contact Legal Services and speak with them about some assistance for you.

'The matter will be heard before a judge of the District Court. You or your solicitor will be given an opportunity to question witnesses and the judge will ultimately make a decision. Since this is a civil matter, not a criminal trial, there will be no jury. Is that okay?' Master Berry inquired.

'To me? I'm not going to agree with you,' Mercuri protested. 'I am totally against this. Obviously, I have no say in the matter.'

The Master patiently explained the situation again. 'The plaintiff has issued a summons. It has taken its course through the trial list. It is now listed for trial. It has been in the trial list since May of this year. The trial date is now coming up in the next couple of weeks. It will be necessary for you to make arrangements to be here.'

'Can I appeal the decision?' Mercuri inquired.

'You have the right to appeal against a decision of a master to a judge. You will need to deal with this as a matter of urgency and you will have to come to Adelaide to prosecute the appeal yourself or have somebody represent you.'

There was an ominous silence on the other end of the line. 'At the moment, the matter is in the trial list on 11 October. I will not make an order taking it out of that list. You will be expected to attend unless some other orders are made by someone else in the meantime,' Master Berry said.

The telephone conference was over and Master Berry formally ordered Mercuri's application to vacate the trial date be dismissed and notification be sent to Mercuri of the new orders. The conference was adjourned. We had gained a small victory.

I suspected the entire judicial system would be glad when the civil action was over. It seemed to be a thorn in everybody's side. The following morning *The Advertiser* ran the headline, 'Mercuri trial to go ahead: Civil sequel to murder case'.[19] Michael Owen-Brown reported that Master Berry had told Mercuri, 'You have put everyone in a very difficult situation. I'm afraid you will just have to come.'

Only ten days to go before District Court record books could be changed forever. Would a history-making precedent be set? Would Mercuri appeal the Master's decision in the meantime? Would my health hold out and what would the consequences be for my future? Only time would tell.

During the six and a half years since Shirree's untimely death I had spent much time waiting. I waited for ten long days for Shirree's body to be released from the coroner's office before she could be laid to rest. I waited over two years for news that the police were ready to make an arrest. I waited another year before the accused was extradited from Victoria. I waited almost another year before the first of the court proceedings, the committal hearing, and a further seven months before Shirree's accused murderer stood trial in a criminal court.

After my decision to instigate the civil action, I again waited. Nineteen months had passed since the acquittal. I'd spent more than six and a half years waiting for justice. But the final ten days before the civil action felt like the longest wait of all. I hadn't realised time could pass so slowly. I didn't sleep, couldn't eat and I couldn't shake the feeling that with each passing minute I was heading for another disastrous disappointment.

It had become obvious to me since my return from Queensland that Mercuri had manoeuvred himself into a position of power. I didn't know whether Mercuri was receiving advice from his usual legal source but he was getting advice from somewhere and had put together a clever strategy. His plan to delay the trial had recently hit a rather large snag but I could not trust him not to come up with something new. After all, Mercuri was fighting to exonerate himself. The onus for proving the case against him was vastly different to that in a criminal court. This time he could not appear as he had in the Supreme Court, innocent until proven guilty beyond any reasonable doubt. This time his sordid criminal history was in the open.

My lawyers still had to prove probability, not an easy task given the past record of unreliability of some of the witnesses. But the balance had shifted a little more in my direction and it seemed Mercuri was not going to find it as easy to circumvent the system.

I didn't trust the system though, and the closer the trial date came, the more apprehensive I was. I felt an ominous black cloud forming around me and I couldn't shake the feeling. I discussed my fears in depth with my doctor and lawyers. They had conflicting opinions as to what I should do. On the one hand the lawyers were of the opinion I should continue with the case and I understood their point of view. On the other hand, my doctor was quite alarmed about the state of my health. There had been a marked change, a definite deterioration to my frame of mind since she'd last seen me. 'My biggest concern is that he'll turn up without a lawyer and if he does that he'll turn the court into a circus,' I told Dr Williams. 'No judge can rule properly under those circumstances.'

'How long have you been worried about this?'

'I've had it on my mind now for at least six months. I've tried not to worry about things that may never happen. How many times have you advised me not to think too far ahead? But I can't help it. The closer the trial gets, the more stunts that bastard pulls and the more slaps in the face I get, the more convinced I am that I'm right.'

'Have you discussed it with Morry and Andrew?'

'Yes, a few times.'

'And their reaction?'

'They're hoping he'll just give up and not bother to show. I'm not so sure. Why would he fight so hard all this time and then just give up when the trial is so close. It's his last shot at exonerating himself. Why would he just give up? Would you, if you were in his shoes? You know I wish I wasn't so convinced he did it. I'd never have started this in the first place if I weren't so sure. I seem to be damned if I do and damned if I don't go ahead.'

'I can't tell you what to do. It's still your decision. But you should think about what it will cost you in terms of the consequences to your health. I don't like what I see and I don't like what I am hearing. And what would it matter if you discontinued now? I know it will be a tough decision to make at this late stage but in terms of your own well-being I have to advise you to be very clear about what you do.

'Whatever your decision will be, remember your entire future is what is at stake. As I see it, you have to weigh up if continuing will be worth the effort in the end. I'll be discussing the situation with Morry in the near future and I'll try to convey what you've told me today.'

If the trial descended into the farce I feared it might, I was convinced a judge could not possibly find in my favour. I just couldn't get my head around the fact that it looked like Mercuri couldn't get a lawyer and would be defending himself. In my opinion it would just make a mock-ery of the court and that was not what I was seeking. I'd stated many times that I was not trying to bring the justice system down. Basically, I supported the legal system, firmly believing it was one of the better

systems around the world; but I was equally firm in my belief that it needed to be reviewed from time to time.

I didn't have any real answers but I'd had a taste of injustice and didn't
like it. I wanted to show people that the system was not perfect, no system
could be and we should strive for improvement. I wanted safety measures
implemented to allow for independent umpires without blinkers to review
cases where anomalies in the system appeared. I wanted to see the victims
of vicious crimes given the opportunity to have a better hearing. I didn't
want the difficult issues placed in a too-hard basket. I was feeling the pain
of a victim and knew how impossible it was to forget, to put it all aside and
get on with life.

The gap between what I wanted and what was achievable was widen-
ing. It all hinged on whether Mercuri would be represented or indeed
if he was going to turn up at trial or not. There was no way to predict
with any certainty what Mercuri had in mind.

'It would be a great pity if you discontinued now,' Morry advised.
'You've come this far—and what if he doesn't show up? You'll have lost
the chance to say that Mercuri knew he couldn't prove he didn't kill
Shirree. We have enough to fight this, Ken, but it's up to you. Andrew is
a very good QC and will give one hundred per cent.'

'I know he will. You both will. I have no problem with either you or
Andrew. My problem is that if this becomes the farce I'm scared it will,
then Shirree will be the loser. She's already paid the ultimate price with
her life. I cannot ... I won't let two courts say that he is not guilty when
every fibre of my being tells me he is. If there were any doubt in my
mind I would never have started this but ...'

'I understand how you feel, but if you can just hang on for a little longer,
at least until we know if he is going to show. You can pull out any time
after the trial starts if you wish, but at least wait until we know if he is going
to show. You may regret pulling out too early,' Morry urged.

'I'll think about it a little longer. That's all I can guarantee.'

'It's all I need to hear for now.'

✖

I could hardly believe I was back in the Sir Samuel Way Building. The civil action was listed for Court 17. I was apprehensive as I strode toward the elevator with my lawyers. On the way in we passed through a metal detection barrier. An offender had recently leapt out of the dock and threatened court officers and a judge with a pair of scissors and as a result, security had been significantly tightened. One of the sheriff's officers whom I knew from previous visits to the building said, 'Good luck today, Mr Turner.' I smiled, appreciating the encouragement.

I'd made some very difficult decisions in the past few days and the next few moments were going to change the course of my life once more. What occurred in the next thirty minutes depended on whether Mercuri turned up. We still didn't know what his intentions were. No appeal had been lodged against Master Berry's decision. It was still possible Mercuri would decide it was not worth the effort to come. The civil court could not impose any penalty on him as far as a jail term was concerned. Any damages awarded would be incidental. Mercuri didn't have any money or assets and it had never been an action for monetary gain. I only wanted justice for Shirree. My primary reason for pushing myself to the limit through the delays and frustration had been the pursuit of justice, not money.

My mounting apprehension grew because I did not trust the legal system's capability to dispense justice in the case. There seemed to be a reluctance to deal with something new and this case had been dubbed 'history-making' and 'groundbreaking' by the press. There were hopes by some that the justice system would be given a shake-up by what occurred during the case. Legal precedents were not out of the question and other victims tried to be optimistic that the civil action would succeed.

The interior of the courtroom was very small. I couldn't really put my finger on it but there was a sense of foreboding in the air. I couldn't stop shivering and every time I made eye contact with somebody I could see the same nervousness on their faces as I felt inside. The atmosphere was electric. The clock inched slowly toward the starting time. Everyone present waited in hushed anticipation. Mercuri had not arrived. I could feel the hope and expectation around me.

The case was to be tried before Judge John Sulan and was called at precisely 10 am when the Judge took his place at the bench. The tension in the courtroom was evident. His Honour spoke first. 'I gather the defendant is not here. I think we had better call the case.'

A sheriff's officer called the case outside the courtroom. Still no appearance by Mercuri. Andrew Martin QC rose to his feet and addressed His Honour. He requested judgment be made in default of Mercuri's non-appearance at trial and for damages to be assessed.

Judge Sulan questioned whether he should have Mercuri called around the precincts of the court. He asked if the plaintiff had received any form of communication from Mercuri announcing his intentions. Martin told His Honour they had tried to ascertain what Mercuri's intentions were over the weekend without success. Martin reminded His Honour there had been a request for an adjournment from Mercuri. The Judge said he was aware of the application and supporting affidavit.

Judge Sulan appeared reluctant to grant the request for judgment by default and suggested calling Mercuri to find out why he had not appeared. Again I could not help but feel that the court was bending over backwards to cater for Mercuri's 'rights'. He had flagrantly disregarded previous directions by the Masters of the Court in pre-trial conferences and hearings, had employed any tactic he could come up with to delay the proceedings—and the court was still doing all it could to protect his rights. It was as if I had no rights at all. I could not believe the court continued to allow Mercuri to call the shots.

The tension was almost unbearable. I felt like I did in the waiting room at the morgue just before I was asked to identify Shirree's body. It was sort of unreal, like watching a fiction movie. I was only just holding on. There was a huge weight on my shoulders and it was getting heavier by the second. While the Judge decided what he should do the door to the courtroom burst opened. Two young men entered the room, walking toward us. Mercuri and another man had made a dramatic last-minute appearance, ten minutes late.

There was a collective gasp of disbelief from onlookers as he arrogantly announced, 'Sorry I'm late. I'm Frank Mercuri.' Mercuri gave no respectful recognition of the Judge or the Court.

I hid my reaction well, although I was not surprised Mercuri had come. I always felt he would make a last-ditch effort to delay the trial if he was not going to be able to make it. With everything Mercuri had pulled to date, nothing would have surprised me.

'You're Mr Mercuri ... are you?' the Judge asked.

'Yes.'

'We've just called your matter and an application has been made for judgment in default of your appearance. I was just looking at your affidavit. But you're here now so we can proceed.'

'Okay, what do I do?' Mercuri's arrogance and lack of respect for the court astounded every person in the room. It became clear that Mercuri was not going to be represented by counsel. He intended to defend himself.

'You can sit at the bar table, Mr Mercuri,' the Judge told him.

Mercuri and his friend made a big production of spreading their documents across the table.

'I wonder if I might have the benefit of a very short adjournment, just for a couple of minutes, to get instructions,' Morry asked respectfully.

Judge Sulan left the bench and Andrew, Morry and I left the court. I had discussed with Andrew and Morry the possibility of discontinuing the action on a number of occasions but now was the moment I had to decide.

Dr Williams had given her expert opinion about the consequences to my health if I continued the action. She had written a strong letter advising against continuing and Andrew and Morry had prepared a

Notice of Discontinuance in the event that I decided to call a halt to the proceedings. On the other hand, Morry and Brendan had felt there was still a good chance Mercuri might not appear, therefore judgment would be made by default. They'd advised me to try to continue at least until the first day of the proceedings.

But now Mercuri had shown up and I had to make a decision, one of the most important decisions I would ever have to make.

'I can't guarantee anything,' Andrew stated honestly. I looked from Andrew to Morry and back to Andrew again; their expressions were grim. I didn't have to guess what they were thinking. I knew they wanted me to continue but I also knew I could not. My mind was working overtime to find just one reason to continue. On the one hand I didn't want Mercuri to think he had won hands down but on the other hand I really didn't care anymore. It all came down to what Shirree would have wanted me to do. I felt she would have known that I had done all I could under the circumstances. I knew she would not be pleased if I became so ill that I would be of no use to anybody let alone myself. I had made my decision.

'Pull the pin,' I said decisively. 'I cannot continue under these circumstances. He'll turn this into a circus. I won't let him do that to Shirree.'

'Are you certain that's what you want,' Morry said. 'Once we go in there and table the Notice of Discontinuance you won't be able to change your mind.'

'I know. Let's get it over with,' I said.

I felt I was letting so many people down, especially Andrew and Morry who had put so much time and hard work into the preparation of the trial. Now all their work seemed to be in vain. They thought they stood a very good chance of success in obtaining the justice I desired for Shirree, but to me it now seemed impossible. I felt that Judge Sulan was in an untenable situation. He would not have been able to make a fair decision. If Mercuri was unable to adequately defend himself then I was not prepared to allow him to turn the proceedings into a circus. I would not have been able to live with two courts finding in Mercuri's favour just because in the first instance there was not enough admissible evidence to convict and in the second he was not properly represented. I could not allow Mercuri to tell the world that not one, but two courts said he was innocent when I believed the opposite.

The Supreme Court said Mercuri was not guilty because there are only two possible verdicts—guilty or not guilty. Just because Mercuri was acquitted did not mean he did not commit the crime. There was not enough evidence to prove guilt beyond reasonable doubt. Doubts about the court's ability to dispense justice were justified this time, but only because Mercuri didn't have legal representation.

We returned to the courtroom, all three of us grim-faced. I sat stiffly at the bar table waiting for Judge Sulan to return to the bench. We decided to alert Mercuri about what we intended to do before the Judge returned. His Honour stayed in chambers for a full thirteen minutes before Andrew Martin rose to his feet and delivered my instruction citing the plaintiff's failing health and tabling a letter from Dr Williams to support the application. Mercuri appeared puzzled, yet relieved. Morry wasn't sure Mercuri understood the implications.

After discussion about the legal implications His Honour asked, 'Do you have anything to say on the matter, Mr Mercuri?'

'Are you Master Berry?' Mercuri asked indignantly.

'No. I'm Judge Sulan. You are now in front of a judge.'

'Well, I don't know how it works,' Mercuri complained.

'I know you don't and I don't expect you to,' the Judge said patiently. Mercuri spent the next few minutes complaining bitterly about how put out he was. It was as if he didn't understand what had happened.

Judge Sulan explained again that if leave were granted to discontinue, it would be on the condition that I could not to bring another action involving the same subject matter.

'I'd be for that. I wouldn't oppose that,' Mercuri said.

'I'm sure you wouldn't oppose that,' the Judge commented.

'I'd be fully for that, as long as that's the judgment.'

'Well, that's the order I intend to make.'

'That's very kind. Thank you. That's how I would like it.'

The Judge ordered me to pay the defendant's costs and suggested Mercuri work out his costs and out-of-pocket expenses. 'I just want a ticket home,' Mercuri said. Judge Sulan explained he would have to work it out with my lawyers.

'If you can't agree then the court will sort it out.'

'How am I going to get back to Melbourne? Can you point me in the right direction to get help for that?' Judge Sulan patiently explained he should see my solicitor and if a resolution could not be worked out then he should retain a lawyer to assist him.

'Nobody seems to want to come anywhere near me to represent me,' Mercuri continued to complain. The Judge explained the court could not provide him with a lawyer and he should go to Legal Aid and see if they could assist him.

Judge Sulan suggested one more time that Mercuri retain a lawyer to explain the consequences of what he was about to do and gave the order to end the action. 'I grant leave for the plaintiff to discontinue. The plaintiff's claim is therefore dismissed. I grant leave on the condition the plaintiff is not to bring any further action against the defendant in respect of the subject matter of the action now before this court, which I now dismiss. There will be an order for the plaintiff to pay the defendant's costs to be agreed upon.'

As Andrew and Morry gathered papers together and packed them into briefcases I was aware of the media leaving the court to phone in the result for the evening news. They would never know what the result might have been had I continued but I felt peaceful about my decision.

It was finally over. As far as the court was concerned the law books were closed on the Shirree Turner murder forever. The action, such as it was, had taken a little over thirty minutes and in effect the result would be entered into the court annals as a 'no finding' verdict.

Morry told me that Mercuri had asked about the bus ticket. 'I told him to send the details of his costs, in the form of an account, to my office and I'll take care of it,' Morry said. I was relieved I didn't have to deal with Mercuri in person. I'd had enough for one day but it was not over yet.

Mercuri must have been relieved when the civil action ended. He did not have to defend himself any longer and he would never have to face court over Shirree's murder again.

A few days later Fiona Clark of Channel Ten *Eyewitness News* secured a lengthy interview with Frank Mercuri. During the interview, Mercuri claimed he had been branded as a 'a killer for life' and he believed the system had left him a 'marked man'.

'Even though our system all too often leaves victims of crime and their families feeling let down, there are two sides to every story. Do you think that people think you are a killer?' Fiona asked.

'Hundred per cent … without a doubt,' Mercuri replied. When Fiona implied that he was charged because of the stories of Schinella and Thallas, Mercuri said he was not the type of person to go to the police making 'shonky reports, saying that he had heard someone saying this and that'. He said he had 'no explanation why they [Thallas and Schinella] would do that'.

'Frank Mercuri is the first to admit he's no angel. He's spent most of his life in jail but like every accused he came to South Australia to face trial with the presumption of innocence and the jury took less than two hours to find him "not guilty". Six months later, Shirree Turner's father launched an unprecedented legal action suing Mr Mercuri for the killing of his daughter. At issue was the fact that the jury was not told that in 1994 Mercuri stabbed and tried to rape a female friend,' Fiona reported.

'I mean, all right, a crime was committed. I paid for that. How much more do I have to pay and what for?' Mercuri responded.

'The Turner case has renewed cries for previous convictions to be put to juries, something always considered to bias a trial. To use them now, the law says the facts must be similar. Mr Mercuri's Victorian lawyer said that the offences were worlds apart,' Fiona continued.

'In reality, there are quite marked differences between stalking a woman in the street who was a complete stranger and someone being raped on a date,' Mercuri's Victorian lawyer remarked in the interview.

I was astounded. Caroline had been coerced by Mercuri into going to his motel room for a drink on New Year's Eve. She had already arranged plans for the evening, but Mercuri was not going to take no for an answer. I could not believe a lawyer could infer that Caroline's innocent encounter with Mercuri was considered a date rape. And I doubted Caroline would have considered the meeting a date either.

Fiona continued her report, stating that I had withdrawn the action as soon as Mercuri arrived in court. Mercuri claimed I never intended to let him have his say. 'When I walked through those doors I saw the look on their faces and they were fully disappointed and they quit, not me. We can use the justice system as it is or we can invent a few roundabouts and side streets to get around it a little bit, to get to people. And that's the wrong way to conduct the law,' Mercuri claimed.

'Now it's left him with the stigma of being thought a killer,' Fiona stated. 'It's cost him two jobs and a home and left him as the Victorian Rape Squad's prime suspect for unsolved attacks. All over a crime for which he was never convicted.'

Fiona asked one final question. 'Did you kill Shirree Turner?'

'No, and I believe I've done enough to prove that,' was Mercuri's reply.

Had I heard him correctly? He had done enough to prove he had not killed Shirree? I wondered exactly what he had done to prove his innocence. Did he produce the knife Thallas gave him to prove it was the double-edged knife given as the gift? Did he come up with an airtight alibi for the night in question?

I was furious after watching this interview. What exactly had Frank Mercuri done to prove his innocence? Nothing. He hadn't had to prove a thing.

Epilogue
Not a Fairytale Ending

There is no fairytale ending to this story. This is not a fiction story where the good guy wins and rides off into the sunset. This was a true story and in real life we have to accept what appears to be less than ideal. It may appear to some that I went after Mercuri but that was the very last thing on my mind. My motives were purely to seek justice for Shirree. I knew from the beginning that I had nothing else to gain.

If Frank Mercuri had been properly represented in the Civil Court there would have been a different ending to this story. It would have afforded me the opportunity of presenting the truth, the information not admissible in the first trial. It would have given the court a fair fight to adjudicate over. But I had felt the devastation of injustice before and my own wellbeing meant more to me than risking another injustice. Who knows what the consequences would have been had I decided differently?

There are many reasons for my belief the police 'got it right' when they arrested Frank Mercuri, most of which were not admissible in court or for which there was no corroborating evidence. When the police first received the call from the person subsequently given informant status, they were given specific information. The police were told Mercuri had gone directly to his friends after the murder and several of them were involved in assisting him to dispose of his clothes and the weapon before transporting him from the area. Individuals were named. It was information that could not be ignored. If the information was true, then is it any wonder that these individuals could not tell the truth. They were accessories to the crime of murder.

At about the same time police received a separate call from a different source in another location. Information was given about the murder and what the informant knew. It appeared that this caller knew the informant and knew how scared the informant was.

It is entirely possible Shirree's killer panicked after the attempt to rape her. I believe Shirree would not have been able to identify her attacker because of her degree of intoxication. It is possible he stabbed her in a state of panic. The extent of her injuries suggested it was a frenzied attack. She had ten knife wounds, four of them deep chest wounds. It is also possible that her killer may have aborted the rape attempt and stabbed her in anger or frustration. The police suspected the murder could have been what is termed a 'thrill kill'.

It has always bothered me and those who knew Shirree that she apparently went willingly with a stranger. It was very unusual for her to go anywhere with someone she did not know. Fabio and Evan were convinced she would not have gone with a stranger for any reason, especially when out with friends. She would not have left her friends without telling them.

I cannot dispute the fact that Shirree left the Charles Sturt Tavern. I feel she went outside to get some fresh air and if she had not spoken to the two women she met outside the venue I believe she would have gone back into the Tavern to rejoin her friends. How and when she met her attacker is something I will never know for certain. It has been suggested Shirree knew her killer. Shane Cherry, the security guard from the Princes Berkeley Nightclub, told the court that when Shirree stopped to talk with him she referred to the man she was with as her 'friend'. He also selected Fabio's photograph out of the many he was shown from the folder the police compiled.

The police and several people who did not know Fabio personally noticed a striking resemblance between Mercuri and Fabio. Did Shirree think the man she went with was Fabio? Could she have made a fatal error and gone with her killer, thinking she was safe with a 'friend' who would take care of her, someone she knew who would be happy to take her home? Or could this be just a coincidence?

When Thallas saw Mercuri with a woman in Rosina Street, Thallas said the woman was mumbling in a foreign language. He said he thought it might have been Spanish or French. Thallas was Greek. Could he have recognised the language if it were Italian? Mercuri is Italian. Why would Mercuri ask Thallas what language the woman was speaking? Thallas had to be very careful what he told the police. Why say anything about the woman muttering in a foreign language at all? If the language was Italian why not admit it? He had already told the police that Mercuri had confessed to a murder. Why not tell the police it was an Italian-speaking woman Mercuri was with? It would have added some credence to his story.

During the trial, Defence Counsel asked the question in her closing address, 'If Shirree could speak another language, why was it not introduced into evidence?' I would also like to ask why the question was never asked, either in court or of me. I could have told them Shirree learnt to speak Italian while spending time with Fabio's family and the two women who spoke to Shirree outside the Charles Sturt Tavern mentioned Shirree was speaking with an Italian accent. Another coincidence or did the police overlook this piece of information?

Mercuri stated categorically during the trial that he 'didn't use knives'. What did he use on Caroline when he attacked and stabbed her? He had made too many ambiguous statements. And why didn't Thallas produce the double-bladed knife he said he kept for himself? Perhaps it would have helped validate his story or maybe he felt it would have implicated him as an accessory to the crime.

In a statement given to police, the owner of the Chambers Street apartment said that after Mercuri and Berti vacated the apartment it was left in a very bad state. Not only was there a mess to clean up, substantiated by Julian Berti's mother, but the owner also claimed that the door to the master bedroom had to be replaced because of damage made by knife marks. He said it looked like somebody had thrown a knife at the door several times, like throwing darts at a dartboard.

I had grave doubts the apartment would have been rented to Mercuri and Berti with the master bedroom door in that condition. So who made the knife marks on the back of that door? Coincidentally, it was the very bedroom Mercuri used, the one where the bedside cabinet was, where he placed the birthday knife. Details about the damaged apartment were never introduced into court. Why? Did the police and prosecutor overlook this information?

The acquittal left Detective Johnson and his team shattered. It seemed all their hard work had been in vain. In an interview after the trial Detective Johnson said he did not know why the witnesses turned in court. 'They let the prosecution down. I think they just didn't want to know about it. The jury could see they were having problems and that was the end of it.' Detective Johnson summed it up very well.

When a criminal is acquitted of a crime he has committed he begins to believe he is innocent. To the criminal mind a verdict of not guilty *means* they are not guilty. Questions could be raised about the validity of having only two choices for a jury. There is not enough room for any redress. A guilty verdict can be appealed, but a not guilty verdict is the end of the matter. An offender cannot be tried again in a court of law for the same crime after an acquittal, even if compelling evidence comes to light which points very firmly towards guilt.

Many people now feel that there should be another verdict for a 'not proven' situation, or at least some way for an offender to be charged again if evidence is discovered at a later date. The Scottish legal system allows for a 'not proven' verdict that allows for the possibility for further charges being layed at a later date if fresh evidence is discovered. In Australia, an offender doesn't have to worry after acquittal from the criminal court. He can bask in the fact he will never be tried again on the same charge.

Frank Mercuri left South Australia immediately after Shirree's murder. He left with the knowledge that police in Victoria would soon catch up with him for parole violations. His pattern of behaviour was always the same. When things got too hot he'd lie low for a few months, sometimes in jail, hoping the heat would die down.

Mercuri wasn't interested in talking to police about Shirree's murder and he wasn't interested in talking with police when he found out Caroline survived. He knew he had no choice in that instance so he gave himself up, then refused to talk. Career criminals say, 'Never admit to anything', and Mercuri adhered to that line of thinking.

I will never know the answer to certain questions. Putting together known facts and my suspicions helps me to deal with the fact that Shirree's murder will never be completely solved. The system may have failed me but I would like to state emphatically: the system is not the enemy. The need for change from time to time still exists but I would be the first to say the Westminster system of justice is possibly the best legal system operating in the world.

The principal reason for pursuing the course of justice after Mercuri's acquittal was not born out of a sense of revenge or retaliation. My belief that a killer had been allowed to get away with his crime compelled me to try to do something to bring attention to some parts of the legal system that should be assessed. If I had not pursued justice and just accepted the decision of the criminal court, ignoring the fact that another woman might became a victim of this offender, I could not have lived with myself.

I have tried to be fair about the issues raised. I always wanted this story to portray the effect a murder has on those left to grieve the loss. I hope my experiences and my reactions will give hope to other victims of vicious crimes so that they might come through their experience with some sanity and dignity. There is life after a traumatic experience like murder.

I have come to terms with the fact that there are many unresolved issues in the world and if my experience can help to bring about some small change to the legal system then the past ten years will take on a more acceptable meaning to me.

Since the 2002 election of a new State Government in South Australia, changes have already been implemented. Harsher penalties for crimes such as violent home invasions have been enacted into law and further changes in the area of law and order are currently before parliament. This new pro-active government stood on a platform of reforms to law and has brought initiatives in quickly. The government is listening to the wider community and taking on board the very real concerns brought on by an upsurge of violence in crimes.

I, personally, have decided to continue to lobby government from time to time about issues that I feel need to be looked at. I may only be one voice but my experience will continue to reflect community concerns about finding justice. The Similar Fact Evidence law is a particular thorn in my side. Although I understand the reasoning it is not easy to accept.

Criminals today know how to play the system. They know that even if confronted with a court appearance, Legal Services will provide them with a lawyer. I am not opposed to a person being represented but the balance of the system needs to be taken away from the defendant's favour.

Most people are happy to support measures for rehabilitation but repeat offenders with no regard for life or property should be dealt with harshly. The 'softly softly' approach isn't working and habitual criminals are not concerned about repeating offences. They know that, if caught, they will be provided with an attorney who in most cases will get them a slap on the hand or, at worst, a suspended sentence.

An article published in *The Advertiser* on 9 October 2001 ran the headline, 'Push to reveal past to juries'.[19] It reported that the Government of the United Kingdom was considering giving juries the right to learn about previous convictions of defendants if previous crimes had a direct relevance to the case being tried. The changes were among other recommendations being considered on reforming the justice system.

Senior Appeal Judge, Lord Justice Auld, was commissioned to review the entire criminal justice process and report his findings, as well as suggest proposed changes. Lawyers and civil liberty campaigners were alarmed about hints of what the report contained, and certain to oppose the proposed changes.

Other leaked information contained a proposal for judges to order a retrial if they believed a jury's acquittal of a defendant was perverse. Outraged lawyers said the report struck at the heart of the jury system and exposing a defendant's previous convictions would lead to prejudice against the accused.

I was pleased to hear the proposed changes will not be rejected out of hand and trust that any changes made to the English justice system, on which our Australian legal system is modelled, will eventually filter into the Australian system.

A Word from the Author

Halfway to Justice is the true story of a father's love for his daughter. Ken Turner had to endure what must be every parent's worst nightmare. His twenty-two-year-old daughter, Shirree Ann, was wrenched from his life in the early hours of Sunday 6 June 1993 in one of the most callous ways imaginable.

When Ken asked me to consider writing the book I was flattered. I have been a reader for most of my life and it is every avid reader's dream to write a book. Few are handed the opportunity and the awesome responsibility only became evident when I realised the seriousness of the challenge. At the time of completing the manuscript, it has been more than ten years since Shirree Ann Turner was murdered.

The task of sifting though the information has by no means been an easy one. I did not know too much more about this story than the average person who read newspaper accounts and viewed television news reports. Ken moved to Queensland a year after the murder, expecting to return after the Supreme Court trial. He came to live in my home temporarily and I had the privilege of helping him by typing letters and assisting with research into matters of law.

Ken was very open and willing to share his feelings from the start and didn't hold back. I have been 'crawling around inside Ken's head' for more than five years and have been trusted with almost unlimited access to his innermost thoughts. The trust placed in me to put those thoughts on paper was an awesome responsibility and I hope I have fulfilled the responsibility well. The story is unique. Some of the legal matters have never before been attempted in Australia. What we set out to achieve in relating the story is threefold.

Firstly, we seek to bring to young people, particularly women, the truth about the dangers of living in society today. The attitude 'it will never happen to me' is fraught with peril. Young people are vulnerable, not invincible, and there are evil predators who prey on the vulnerable and lonely.

Secondly, we seek to ask the justice system to look at putting safety measures in place to ensure that when a violent crime is committed offenders will not find it as easy to 'beat the system'. A bit of commonsense will go a long way toward lifting faith in the justice system. A victim's rights are equally as important as an offender's.

Thirdly, we seek to show some idea of the utter anguish and almost indescribable emotional trauma felt by the family and close friends of a victim of vicious crime. The inner pain for the closest loved ones is profound, in some cases inconsolable, for most a never-ending battle—a life sentence.

The bulk of information regarding court trials came from transcripts of the various hearings, together with copies of statements and other documents pertaining to the issues raised in the manuscript. Some of the material was not pleasant to view or read. The report from the coroner's office, which described what happened to Shirree in graphic detail, and photographs from the crime scene and autopsy, only confirmed what I had imagined in my mind.

Ken has not been able to view the photographs himself and he is well aware of the enormous responsibility he placed on my shoulders. He knew what an awesome task it would be to piece together the entire story and in accepting the challenge I experienced much of the same sense of outrage that close family and friends did. The jury was shown a selection of the same photographs and asked to view them 'dispassionately'. Ken and I have trouble in accepting a dispassionate view can be taken of such material. Have we become so desensitised that a judge, warning a jury that what they are about to see will be unpleasant, can still ask them to view it 'dispassionately'? Is it assumed that we are so indifferent to violence and crime that we can do this without feeling or emotion? Or was this unemotional viewing of shocking material expected of the jury because they did not know Shirree personally and would be impervious to any feeling or emotion?

Ken knows he has done all he can for Shirree in the pursuit of justice. The family, Shirree's friends, Brad and Ken, will never forget who she was or anything about the part she played in their lives. She will live on through the beautiful memories made together during her short life.

Writing the book has been therapeutic for Ken. He came to realise he has a duty and a responsibility to fight against injustice, for if we do not speak out when we feel something is wrong, we lose the right to complain.

Ken continues to fight injustice and is preparing a testimony to share with youth groups, high school and university students. He has a passion to alert young people to the danger of apathy toward personal safety and stands firm in his resolve to continue to lobby the government.

Ken's family, friends and those with intimate knowledge of what they believe occurred in the early hours of 6 June 1993 have the satisfaction of at least reaching halfway to justice.

The week before the civil action was due to begin Ken asked me to formulate the following statement in the event that he made the momentous decision to abort the civil action. It is appropriate to end the manuscript with this statement. It reads:

After an acquittal from the criminal justice system I decided to pursue justice in a civil court. Recently I have learned that in some cases justice in human courts can fail. I believe firmly in a just God. He will bring correct justice in an unjust worldly circumstance. It may not be as I think it should be, but it will be perfect justice. And it will not be any halfway measure.

To family and friends who constantly encouraged me and allowed me to bury myself in the work, I thank you from the bottom of my heart for your patience, support and constructive criticism, for without dedicated friends and family I doubt I could have finished the manuscript. To you, Ken, belongs gratitude beyond anything I can put into words for your trust, patience and encouragement.

For each of you who has the privilege of being a parent, we cannot impress upon you too strongly to take good care of your children, no matter what age. They are our most precious resource and worthy of extra special love and care.

Finally, I would like to dedicate this manuscript to victims of crime everywhere and to a quite remarkable young lady, Shirree Ann Turner. I did not have the pleasure of knowing Shirree when she was alive, but I know her very well now. I have been permitted to meet Shirree through the eyes of the person who knew her best.

—*Lesley Turner*

 # Endnotes

Chapter 3: A Public Goodbye

1. 'Murder link to city clubs', *The Advertiser*, 8 June 1993, p.1.
2. 'Girl's murder: heartbroken father blames ... An enemy of God', *The Advertiser*, 9 June 1993, p.1.
3. 'Goodbye Shirree', *The Advertiser*, 17 June 1993, pp.1–2.
4. 'Shirree: A loving life that ended in tragedy', *The Advertiser*, 12 June 1993, p.1.
5. 'Major crime squads fully stretched: public afraid to help police solve murders', *The Advertiser*, 12 June 1993, p.11.

Chapter 4: A Kind of Healing

6. 'Sad plea for a murdered friend', *The Advertiser*, 19 March, 1994, p.4.

Chapter 13: The Verdict

7. 'So who killed Shirree?', *The Advertiser*, 18 March 1998, p.3.
8. 'Exposed: the dark side of Frank Mercuri', *The Advertiser*, 21 March 1998, p.1.

Chapter 14: Pursuing Justice

9. 'The daughter I'll never forget', *The Advertiser*, 28 March 1998, p.23

Chapter 15: Media Attention

10. 'Father sues man cleared of murder', *The Advertiser*, 14 September 1998, p.3.
11. 'Flashbacks to a nightmare', *The Advertiser*, 15 September 1998, p.15.
12. 'Attempted rape conviction "pertinent to case" ', *The Advertiser*, 15 September 1998, p.15.
13. 'Australia's first OJ Simpson trial', *Woman's Day*, 21 September 1998, pp.14–15.
14. Full transcript taken from *A Current Affair*, Channel Nine, first broadcast 15 September 1998.

Chapter 16: Politics and the Law

15. 'Denial on killing', *The Advertiser*, 31 October 1998, p.28.
16. 'God's gift to me: Why Ken Turner fights for justice over the murder of his daughter', *The Advertiser*, 18 May 1999, p.10.
17. 'A difficult question of judgment', *The Advertiser*, 29 July 1999, p.16.
18. The circular of the Attorney-General, 'The admissibility of previous convictions', Trevor Griffin, 3 August 1999.

Epilogue: Not a Fairytale Ending

19. 'Push to reveal past to juries', *The Advertiser*, 9 October 2001, p.22.